Counseling and Therapy Skills

Overcome Anxiety and Improve Relationships

Katerina Burns

Copyright © 2019 - All rights reserved.

Table of Contents

Introduction

Understanding Who You Really Are

"Who am I?" This is our initial question, and it's an important one, because "To know thyself is the beginning of wisdom."

This famous quote, often attributed to Socrates, the classical Greek moral philosopher whose work is the foundation for Western Philosophy, will be our starting point.

The importance of intimately knowing who you are and being able to identify yourself as an individual of worth is perhaps the keystone to successfully managing your own emotions and being able to lead a peaceful, happy, and productive life.

So, how do you discover who you really are?

Each individual wears multiple hats throughout their lifetime. You were born a son and given a name to identify you from others in your family and community. You became a friend to someone, then perhaps a student at university, followed by becoming a colleague at your place of work. Thereafter, you may have graduated to become a husband, a brother-in-law, and then you became a father. You may also be a brother and an uncle. For each role you play in life, you show a different side of yourself. Despite the roles you play and sides you show. You are still you, an intricate creation of many parts and dimensions.

Each step of your life takes you through stages of personal growth and development common to all humanity. The single constant throughout your life is your name, and your name, eternally linked to your inner spirit, identifies you as the individual personality you truly are.

All the struggles, setbacks, suffering, and heartache you endure during your lifetime could be linked to you neither being fully aware nor accepting who you are. Knowledge of your inner being includes an honest awareness and acknowledgment of your strengths and weaknesses. Armed with this insight into your intimate self, you will be better prepared to manage your emotions and understand their root causes. With this understanding comes the innate awareness of who you really are and the consciousness of how best to resolve your emotional conflict through the development of valuable skills.

In Eastern cultures, individuals are exhorted to carefully examine themselves to discover their true inner being. This intimate exploratory process takes time and patience, but the result is worth the effort, namely the clear understanding of who you are and what you wish to achieve from your life.

In Western countries, individuals are not afforded the same opportunity to become introspective, but rather tend to compare themselves to others. This comparison, in turn, leads many people of Western origin to accept the superficial things in life, which are often of a material nature, like smart cars or name-brand clothing, and to use these items as the benchmarks of their personal success.

The critical aspect of your quest to discover your true identity is to remember that you are an individual in your own right. You are the hero in your own life story. It is, therefore, your responsibility and indeed your duty to make your best effort to live your life to its fullest.

How Self-Knowledge Can Benefit You

The more in-depth knowledge we have about ourselves, the better prepared we will be to deal with our emotions, and consequently, our thoughts as well as our actions.

The search for the essence of self may be the foundation for inner knowledge that will eventually lead to a more fulfilling existence and allow us to make sense of life.

The following points are suggestions that may be of value when considering who you really are:

Searching for happiness

Happiness is an emotion closely linked to our sense of well-being and comfort. It is a personal state of mind and inner spirit. This state is fundamental to a productive, successful, and viable lifestyle without which, individuals are less likely to function to their optimum level or achieve their goals for prosperity. By expressing who you really are, you open the door for others to get to know you and to interact with you in a positive and meaningful manner. This is not always an easy task, as most of us are somewhat reluctant to expose our true selves to others for fear of failure, ridicule, or unexpected manipulation.

To be truly happy is indicative of your self-confidence, total acceptance of self, and the knowledge of who you are at heart. Happy people enjoy being in their own skin and are satisfied and content with their lot in life. They generally have a good idea of their strengths and acknowledge their weaknesses but seldom allow these any control over their lives.

So how do you find happiness? Try the following ideas:

- ❖ Hang out with people who are happy and make you smile.
- ❖ Value and respect your own values.

❖ Accept all the good things that happen in your life, no matter how small or insignificant they may appear.

❖ Visualize the best happening to you. Positive thoughts bring positive events and actions.

❖ Participate in things you love doing as often as possible.

❖ Find your purpose in life and a place where you feel valued.

❖ Listen to the messages your heart sends you and remember there are others in your family and social group who only want the best for you.

❖ Take responsibility for your own fulfillment and don't blame others for your situation.

❖ Accept change even though it may not make you feel good at first. Because change is inevitable in life, you need to learn to 'roll with the punches' and adapt.

❖ Enjoy the simple pleasures in life, such as having a loving family to share fun times and make wonderful memories with (Goldsmith, 2012).

Experiencing less inner conflict

When you are able to act and interact in accordance with your true personal feelings, you are less likely to experience inner conflict and, therefore, more likely to enjoy greater peace of mind. A clear understanding of your strengths and limitations will assist you in understanding how you feel and how you should function for optimum success in your home, at your place of work, and in society in general. Self-knowledge brings about a clearer understanding of what really matters to you and what brings you inner peace.

Being equipped to make better decisions

Decision making is a vital aspect of our lives, the importance of which is sometimes overlooked and undervalued. Knowing yourself intimately will help you to make decisions that are right for you. Self-knowledge ensures you are less likely to be manipulated by others into making incorrect choices, whether these be minor in nature, such as deciding on which shoes to wear or major such as choosing a life partner or purchasing a property.

In any family, the best gifts parents can bestow on their children is the knowledge and skills to make sound, well-thought-out decisions in their lives. Humans were born with freedom of choice, which most of us exercise without much thought, on a daily basis. When choices are made based on emotional factors, we are likely to flounder sooner or later, in the resulting quagmire.

Improved self-control

Through in-depth self-knowledge, you will be more likely to demonstrate better self-control, and, with the development of improved self-control comes a better understanding of who you are and an increased awareness of the importance of retaining your composure during stressful events. Self-restraint is not an easy thing to exercise, as we are all emotionally based individuals who often respond impulsively to the conflicting and sometimes confusing stimuli we are bombarded with on a daily basis. By developing your composure, you can become better equipped and prepared to recognize your responses to these circumstances and to alter your reactions accordingly. Self-control encourages you to be less hasty and more conscious of the consequences of your actions.

Children can be naturally impetuous and sometimes thoughtless in their actions. Parents who exercise self-control act as good role models for their children. The children will learn by example the acceptable responses to difficult situations.

Resisting social pressures

Possessing good self-knowledge enables you to overcome the temptations exerted by social pressures. Instead of feeling obliged to accept advances you don't enjoy or agree to a decision you find unpleasant, you can step back and be more objective and exercise your own willpower. Social pressures play an integral role in creating and maintaining high levels of stress and anxiety in our lives. The cleverly coercive tactics from a variety of media sources bombard us to purchase items we do not really need, or to participate in activities deemed fashionable and progressive. Young people, in particular, find it difficult to resist social pressures because they fear to be different, will exclude them from their social group. Well developed self-knowledge can support you in being able to exercise your freedom of choice, and by default, become less easily manipulated by social pressure.

Developing a tolerance for others

Self-knowledge supports your awareness of your challenges and aids you in admitting and confronting your idiosyncrasies. This honest awareness of your short-comings may enable you to accept other people as they are and to treat them with tolerance and understanding. Your self-knowledge empowers you to be less selfish, to act in a more caring manner and to show empathy toward the members in your family, your colleagues at work as well as the people you meet in your daily life.

Pursuing vitality

When you have the power to acknowledge who you are and accept yourself without question, your sense of well-being improves, and your self-confidence grows. You begin to feel more positive and happier in your own skin and are more likely to enjoy an improved lifestyle. With self-knowledge comes the realization of the value of staying healthy and fit, not only on a physical level but mentally and mindfully as well. Your life's experiences become richer and more fulfilling as your vitality improves.

Once you have developed good self-knowledge, you have the power to make every aspect of your life work to your advantage. The positive spin-off of healthy, well-developed self-knowledge to all areas of your life, from personal relationships and work-related matters to your social life and everything in between, cannot be underestimated.

Chapter 1: The Search for True Meaning in Life

You may wonder what the true meaning of life entails, and whether, in fact one really exists. To be perfectly honest, there may not be a cut and dried answer to these questions.

Throughout time, humans have attempted to discover the reason for their existence on Earth, not only in basic terms of procreation and the process of living and dying, but also in terms of their personal value to a greater good.

This book will not focus on the religious reasons for man's existence, though these have value in the overall search for the meaning in life. There may be no predetermined purpose for your existence, and therefore your life will only have the meaning you or others accord it.

Throughout life, you have connected with a variety of other individuals, who similarly to you, are searching for their own personal meaning and purpose. Inadvertently, your contact with each of these individuals leaves its mark on them and on you. You are influenced by each of these connections in ways you may not at first recognize and which may bring you either power or pain. You may feel happy and positively motivated or influenced by some of these contacts, while others will cause you sadness, suffering, or confusion and may even lead to feelings of anxiety and depression.

Each interaction we experience is contagious in a manner of speaking, as a little of the other individuals' personalities will rub off on you and influence you in some way. Usually, the positive encounters leave you feeling filled with energy, vitality, and a sense of well-being. You may feel revitalized enough to tackle new ventures and set your sights on attaining greater success.

Is the true meaning of life directly related to what you earn and own, or is it associated with some deeper connection to your mind or soul? Perhaps these questions are too philosophical in nature to find a definitive answer. Consider, just for a moment, what the alternatives might be to placing such great value on material goods, money, or time. What would your priorities be if none of these commodities were an option? You might go into a state of shock and realize that you are unlikely to be able to survive without these items. It might be because you have been raised to believe that time is valuable and inextricably linked to money, which in turn can be utilized to purchase the material goods your heart desires.

Some cultures may emphasize the meaning of life in terms of existential factors like living in isolation, being unable to attribute meaning to your life, fear of death, and man's constant quest for freedom.

Freedom, in essence, refers to that elusive quality many people search fruitlessly for throughout their entire life. To discover the true meaning of life is to determine who you actually are. With this knowledge comes self-acceptance and inner peace.

Ways to Search for the True Meaning in Your life

In order to discover your true inner self (the individual who has a value greater than any precious stones or metals) you will need to ask yourself several searching questions. Once you have completed this personal cross-examination, as honestly as you can, you should prioritize your goals and set about making the changes you want to see to achieve these. Bear in mind, that you and only you are ultimately the 'driver' of your life's vehicle, so your choices are of vital importance to your personal success.

The importance of being happy in your own skin

When you look at yourself in the mirror daily, are you happy with the person you see there? We are not only talking about your own physical reflection but also included here is the inner, private person, with whom you (and only you) are completely intimate with. If you wish to change for the better, improve yourself in any way, you are the only one required to make this conscious decision to bring about the changes you want to see.

Many people are happy and content with themselves. These are usually people who have already developed in-depth self-knowledge and have made the changes they want to see in themselves and are now at peace with themselves because they have discovered their individualized, true meaning of life. Accept yourself for who you are and don't sweat-the-small-stuff.

The importance of creating positive change in your life

Think about the things currently in your life that are not perfect. Perhaps these may include excessive debt, a denigrating relationship, or a self-destroying habit. Now decide to make a concerted effort to begin corrective procedures to bring harmony and balance into your life. By leaving chaos in your life un-checked, it only multiplies and increases your anxiety and depression.

Many individuals long to be able to change some aspect of their lives, whether this is of a financial, physical, or intellectual nature. Some people may measure their own success, or lack thereof, by other people's acquisitions or status, which often appear provocative and create an ardent desire in us to emulate.

Ask yourself what specific thing or action do you want to change? Do you long for wealth and financial stability, a better job, more affluent friends, a new vehicle, or the latest most up-to-date electronic device? Or perhaps your desires include a quieter lifestyle, a loving relationship, well-behaved children, and a peaceful, harmonious home life? Whatever changes you would like to implement in your life, will depend on how willing you are to adapt your thought patterns and actions to achieve your desired aims. Nothing good comes from inaction, so if you want to see the change, you need to make it happen.

Gratitude is the key to a happy life

Thankfulness is a positive emotion that results in feelings of satisfaction and peace. Think of all the things for which you are grateful. Include your physical environment, a roof over your head, a warm, safe place to sleep, food to eat, perhaps the amenities of clean water and electricity, clothes and footwear, access to medical care, and transport. Now think of the relationships that you value. These may include family, friends, colleagues, and neighbors.

There is a lot to be thankful for, and it is important to look for all the positive aspects of your life. Take note of these and be grateful for them. Contentment can grow and flourish from this seed of gratitude. Many people who may be less fortunate than you, may rejoice at the fact they have somewhere to sleep and perhaps a daily meal.

Whatever your circumstances, acknowledging your gratitude will add value to your search for the true meaning of life and will bring you a sense of inner peace.

Kindness and helpfulness add meaning to life

Being alive presupposes interaction and interconnection with everything around you, and there is an understanding that you cannot live successfully in a vacuum. Every individual you meet during your day presents, as you do, an exterior version of themselves to the world. Their inner, personal self is generally not displayed for fear of reprisal or condemnation or perhaps simply because they are too shy to wear their hearts on their sleeves. When you meet new people as you go about your daily life, you see only their exterior. Each individual carries their own burdens; some may be noticeable while others are well hidden.

In order to further your search for true meaning in life, you need to be prepared to acknowledge these individuals for who they are and be willing to extend a helping hand where needed. Perhaps you could offer up your seat on the train to that pregnant woman or senior citizen, compliment someone on their excellent service, make that call to your elderly parent, or visit a sick friend. Every act of kindness, either random or planned, brings pleasure to both the giver and the recipient and supports the establishment and development of your positive emotional and mental state. Besides, showing kindness and care toward others gives meaning to your life.

Do people's opinions of you really matter?

At some point in your life, there will be concern about what other people may think about you, your clothes, your choice of home, the car you drive, where you take your vacation, to which school you send your children, and even about the way you walk, talk, behave and live your life.

Young people are particularly affected by what their peers think of them. With the added power and indirect influence of the mass media, peer pressure has increased to the extent that its effect on our children has reached epidemic proportions. It behooves parents to be aware of the challenges modern children face and to offer them support and advice on how to best manage these difficulties, instead of chastising them for making incorrect decisions.

The value of investing in your relationships

How important are your relationships with your family, friends, and colleagues? True happiness and inner peace can be found in loving relationships in which you are accepted and appreciated for the individual that you are. It can be said that no matter your wealth or station in life, without love and companionship, your life is incomplete.

What are the biggest errors you have made in life?

Every human has made errors of some kind during their lifetime. Some of the misjudgments may have caused them great sadness or harm, while others were hugely embarrassing. No matter the magnitude of the error, the fact remains that not a single individual can escape this scenario. We should take stock of our mistakes, learn from them, and move on with a positive outlook while making a conscious effort not to repeat the same gaffes.

Does anxiety play an important role in your daily life?

For most of us, stress and anxiety play an integral part in our lives. Whether we worry about our financial status or family issues, what other people think of us, or if our boss is happy with our efforts, we all agonize over something. If anxiety rules your life, it's time to take stock and make a decision to change your lifestyle for the better.

The importance of recreational activities in your life

Do you have sufficient time in your life for recreation and relaxation? If this question is difficult to answer, your work-fun balance is way out of kilter. Recreation feeds the soul, body, and mind with new ideas, and these opportunities to rest help you to reclaim some much needed healthy vitality. The importance of discovering the balance between your career and leisure activities is part of the secret to your success in life. Leisure time and sleep are essential aspects of a healthy lifestyle.

Happiness and inner peace are two essential emotions existing in tandem, that appear to elude most people. The good news is, if you have found one, you are probably exposed to the other. You, as well as all those who know you, will be richer for this experience.

How do you think your obituary will read?

Have you ever thought about what people might say about you once you are dead? Think back to the obituaries you may have read. Many are glowing reports of people who did well, achieved their goals, and were loyal and honest individuals whose loved ones cared deeply for them. Some obituaries simply mention the name of the deceased and state their date of birth and death.

If you want to be remembered, you need to achieve something remarkable in the eyes of those who look up to you. You need to be prepared to step out of your comfort zone to search for your true meaning in life.

Your Reality Is Specific

Your life and self-knowledge are specific to you and only you. Every person, whether by miraculous accident or divine design, is an individual in their own right. Each of us experiences reality in our own way. To understand the true meaning of life is to witness this phenomenon as an individual dimension of our lives that has collective implications and to simply accept it for what it is.

Each individual is obliged to travel their own life path, either alone or in a partnership, and to learn from their errors as they each work toward developing their peace of mind through ultimate acceptance of their individuality.

Perhaps, the true meaning of life can be summed up succinctly, even though it is a complex and marvelous event, as: Life means what you want it to mean.

Chapter 2: The Value of the Professional Counselor

In order to overcome difficulties that impede your successful progress, you will primarily need to consider your strengths and limitations. Armed with this knowledge, you will be empowered to set upon a suitable course of action to either nullify the negatives or, better still, replace each of these with a strong and meaningful positive. In some cases, where you feel insufficiently capable of assisting yourself, it may be beneficial to seek the advice of a professional counselor to guide you in your endeavors to improve your skills to overcome anxiety and improve your relationships.

To understand the destructive impact anxiety can have on the individual, let us look at the following possible scenario of a young mother who is plagued by stress that impacts negatively on her daily life. She becomes so unhappy and anxious that she loses the confidence to tackle daily chores such as shopping, dropping her children at school as well as the ability to communicate adequately with her partner. If she fails to recognize the symptoms of anxiety and seek professional support, she will continue her downward spiral into self-destruction.

Being 'in-tune' with yourself will likely mean you do not require the support of a counselor. However, if you hit a rough patch and the wheels fall off your wagon, as they will at some point or another in everyone's life, then professional support is definitely an option to consider.

Counseling

The importance of counseling, which usually takes place face-to-face, is the support and guidance offered by a professional to an individual to assist them with their healing process. The counselor endeavors, through the collection of data, to listen to the patient, judge the severity and extent of their problems, and to offer suitable advice and next steps. The objective of counseling is to bring about positive change in the patient's mental or emotional state, which will result in a transformation in their attitude.

In order for any form of counseling to be successful, the patient has to acknowledge the personal or psychological matter of concern that is negatively impacting their life and then be willing to seek professional help. In therapy, the counselor helps the patient to discover the root cause of their problems and to find a solution.

Anxiety disorders differ greatly, so it is therefore essential that the counselor modifies the therapy according to the specific symptoms and diagnosis. The duration of therapy will depend on the severity of the anxiety disorder and may last between eight and 10 weeks. A wide variety of therapies are available for the treatment of anxiety disorders, depending on the specific needs of the patient.

Cognitive-behavioral therapy

We will focus on cognitive-behavioral therapy (CBT) and exposure therapy. Each of these two therapies may either be used alone or in combination and may be conducted individually or in a group. The goal, however, remains the same: to lower the patient's anxiety levels, restore calm to their mind and help them overcome their fear.

Cognitive-behavioral therapy is the most effective and perhaps the most extensively used therapy in the treatment of anxiety and panic disorders as well as phobias. This type of therapy focuses on rectifying the distorted and negative view of their world that patients suffering from these disorders develop. As the name implies, Cognitive-behavioral therapy consists of two important elements:

❖ Cognitive therapy analyzes the impact negative thoughts have on the development and progression of anxiety.

❖ Behavior therapy investigates the individual's reactions and resulting behavior in situations that elicit anxiety.

The basic hypothesis of Cognitive-behavioral therapy is that your thoughts and not external events affect the way you feel and determine your actions. The solution to this dilemma is that you can change the way you feel about a situation simply by altering the way you think about it.

The value of thought challenging in cognitive-behavioral therapy for anxiety

Cognitive-behavioral therapy helps you to challenge and 'restructure' your negative thought processes and replace these with more positive, realistic, and constructive thoughts. This important restructuring process involves three steps:

❖ Identify your negative thoughts

When you suffer from an anxiety disorder, you automatically perceive situations to be more dangerous than they actually are. As it is difficult in most cases for the sufferer to realize the extent of their phobia, a professional therapist may well be able to assist with the process of nailing down the offending cause of the phobia.

❖ Challenge your negative thoughts

At this stage, the therapist, through careful questioning and analysis of data, will advise you of possible tools you can use to measure the negative thoughts that create your feelings of anxiety and panic. The importance of this step cannot be overemphasized as it requires an in-depth look at the causes of your anxiety and fear and gives you an opportunity to recognize these negative thoughts and think of possible solutions.

❖ Replacement of negative thoughts with positive, realistic intentions

Once you have identified your distorted, negative thoughts and predictions, your therapist will guide you towards altering your thought processes to become more positive, objective, and rational. You will also be taught to consistently use calming, refocusing statements or a mantra when you are faced with anxiety-provoking situations.

An example of the thought changing process

To fully understand the process of thought changing, consider the following example: Jane is afraid to use an elevator and will always take the stairs. Her fear of being trapped in an elevator has its roots in her irrational, negative thoughts about being unable to escape from the 'elevator prison' in the event of a mechanical or electrical failure.

When Jane attended therapy to help her overcome her fear, she was requested to write down all her negative thoughts and to identify the cognitive distortions, or errors in her thought process. Once this task was complete, with guidance from her therapist, Jane was able to reconstruct a more positive scenario about traveling in an elevator.

❖ Negative thought #1: What if I am trapped in an elevator?

Cognitive distortion: Believing the worst will happen.

More realistic positive thought: People are not often trapped in elevators.

❖ Negative thought #2: If I am trapped in an elevator, I may suffer a heart attack!

Cognitive distortion: Blowing the entire scenario out of proportion.

More realistic positive thought: I am not likely to suffer a heart attack because I am a young, healthy woman.

❖ Negative thought #3: People will think I am going nuts!

Cognitive distortion: Making unnecessary assumptions.

More realistic positive thought: People are more likely to be concerned about my safety and well-being.

The importance of cognitive replacement therapy lies in its objective to replace negative thinking with more realistic, positive thoughts and ideas. You cannot, however, expect an overnight paradigm shift in your negative thinking, which has been your lifelong thought process pattern. It will take daily practice and a firm commitment to remain focused on changing your negative thoughts to healthy, positive ones. CBT can successfully help you to do the following:

- ❖ Learn to recognize the physical, mental, and emotional symptoms of when you become anxious.
- ❖ Learn proper coping mechanisms and relaxation techniques that will help to alleviate the panic and fear.
- ❖ Try your best to confront your fears using your imagination or seeking the professional support of a therapist.

Exposure therapy for the treatment of anxiety

As anyone who has experienced anxiety will attest to, the fear and unpleasant sensations it causes are no laughing matter. A sure-fire method of cutting down on your anxiety is to avoid the situations you know cause the condition. Aside from the inconvenience, you can, to the best of your ability, live in this state of denial. However, avoidance does not rid you of the problems, which if left unresolved, overtime may reach insurmountable proportions.

Exposure therapy forces you to confront your phobias, fears, and the reasons for your anxiety. Exposure is tackled in one of two ways:

1. Your therapist will support you in imagining frightening scenarios, describing these in as much detail as possible and then working through possible solutions.

2. You may wish to attempt to face real-life situations, which is often extremely difficult to do. Again, however, if this is the therapeutic course of action you choose, you will describe how each situation makes you feel, identify the causes of your anxiety and discuss potential solutions.

The process of exposure therapy usually takes place over an extended period of time, during which you are exposed repeatedly to situations that make you fearful. Gradually it is believed, you will learn to gain control over these situations, which will increase your confidence and decrease your anxiety levels. By confronting your fears, you gain the courage to see them for what they really are and gather the strength to overcome them.

Not everyone, however, has the ability to face their fears head-on. Systematic desensitization is a technique often used by therapists to work through traumatizing situations in a step-by-step process. The premise is that by progressing from mildly threatening scenarios to the worst possible case, allows your mind to cope with smaller bite-sized pieces of the problem and to challenge and master your fears at each level gradually. Only once you have gained control of a specific level, will you be able to progress to the next.

Systematic desensitization involves three important parts:

1. Learning good, functional relaxation skills. You will be required by your therapist to develop progressive relaxation techniques that will help you to breathe deeply and consciously relax every tense muscle in your body. These relaxation skills assist you in overcoming your physical response to fear, such as hyperventilation and shaking.

2. Creating a step-by-step list of frightening situations that cause you fear and anxiety. This task enables you to think of this entire fear process through a series of manageable stages.

3. Working through each and every step under the watchful eye of your therapist. You will begin to realize that many of your fears are unfounded. As you work, each time your anxiety level begins to rise, you will resort to utilizing the relaxation techniques your therapist taught you. Progression is gradual, happening in incremental stages that suit your state of mind and level of progress.

A useful example of a situation that causes a great deal of anxiety in many people is the fear of flying. Your therapist may assist you in this scenario in the following ways:

❖ Asking you to look at and discuss pictures of planes
❖ Inviting you to watch videos of planes taking off, landing or in full flight

- ❖ Suggesting you visit an airport and experience the sounds and visuals of planes in the actual process of taking off and landing
- ❖ Booking a plane ticket, for a short trip
- ❖ Packing your overnight bag and driving to the airport
- ❖ Checking your luggage in and waiting to board your flight
- ❖ Getting onto the plane and actually taking off

Complementary therapies for anxiety disorders

A variety of complementary therapies, suggested to assist in treating anxiety disorders, are available depending on your personal preferences. These therapies are designed to lower your stress and anxiety levels in order to find a better balance in your life (Selig, 2019).

Exercise

Exercise is always the best natural way to eradicate stress. A minimum of thirty minutes of exercise per day, three to five times a week, provides excellent stress relief. The reason exercise works so effectively is because it increases the flow of oxygen-carrying blood to all your muscles as well as your brain.

Relaxation

Relaxation techniques practiced regularly can have a positive impact on the reduction of stress and feelings of anxiety, which in turn has a definite up-swing on your emotional well-being. Techniques such as mindfulness and positive muscle relaxation are valuable tools to consider.

Biofeedback

Biofeedback makes use of special sensors that are attached to various parts of your body. These measure specific physiological processes like your heart rate, breathing, and muscle tension. The premise here is that once armed with this information, you can begin to recognize the symptoms of your body's response to stressful situations and, in turn, begin to take control in a meaningful way through the use of relaxation techniques.

Hypnosis

Hypnosis is a process in which therapeutic techniques are used during your state of deep relaxation, to assist you in identifying underlying causes of your anxiety and then suggesting possible workable solutions.

Chapter 3: Making Anxiety Therapy Work for You

Many people who suffer from anxiety disorders will attest to the fact that there is no 'quick-fix' solution. Therapy support is a worthwhile consideration that involves professional options to assist you in facing your fears rather than doing what many people do, running away from, ignoring or avoiding confronting their disorders.

Anxiety therapy takes time to be effective, so you should be willing to sign-up for the long-term if you want to overcome your anxiety issues successfully. The important thing is that you commit to the treatment and accept your therapist's advice.

You can make a positive personal contribution to your anxiety therapy by recognizing the negative areas in your life and making definitive choices to counteract these with more positive options that will promote inner peace and relaxation. Try to eliminate as much negativity from your life as you can, replacing the negativity with a positive mental attitude that will assist you in identifying the good things in your life and being grateful for these. Happiness and gratitude are two of the cornerstones for good vitality, and they should automatically promote harmony in your life.

If you suffer from anxiety, you are likely to benefit from learning as much as you can about the condition. Knowledge is power, and although education alone may not be the answer to your current challenge, it may certainly provide you with a variety of possible solutions to try.

Remember that loneliness and isolation exacerbate your feeling of inadequacy, which in turn has a negative knock-on effect by increasing your anxiety level. Reaching out to others or accepting their offers of support will be of great value to you. Talking about your feelings and sharing your fears and worries with someone you trust and love can work wonders. Sometimes, just through the act of sharing, we discover potentially positive solutions to our challenges.

Opt for a healthier lifestyle by choosing to participate in daily exercise routines. Watch your eating habits and promote your physical health by avoiding alcohol, nicotine, caffeine, and any drugs, both clinical and recreational.

Try at all costs to avoid stressful situations at home, at work, and in your social sphere. This is perhaps one of the most challenging areas of your anti-anxiety regime to focus on. Stress comes in many forms, and you need to stay alert in order to recognize potential threats to the disruption of your peace and harmony. When you finally destress your life, you will automatically find peace and experience true well-being.

Types of Anxiety Disorders

Therapeutic support is offered for a wide variety of anxiety disorders, which, regardless of the specific disorder, usually have similar underlying patterns. Each disorder can create a sense of despair in the sufferer. There is also an underlying fear of whether you can be helped or if the affliction will worsen and destroy your life. In many cases where anxiety disorders are recognized early, and the correct treatment is administered, there is a good chance of recovery. Some of these anxiety-based disorders are listed below:

Panic disorder

Panic disorder is one of many types of anxiety disorders. It presents in a series of sudden, unexpected, recurring periods of all-consuming fear that result in shaking, shortness of breath, palpitations, and a deep, unexplained sense of foreboding. Panic disorders may appear to the layman to be nothing more than the product of an overactive imagination. For the sufferer, however, these episodes an incredibly real and frightening, and they leave a lasting sense of doom and fear.

If you suffer from regular feelings of suffocating fear that rob you of the ability to think clearly and rationally, you are possibly suffering from a panic disorder. Attacks of this nature are usually fairly short, lasting between five and 10 minutes. The exact causes are not known but there is a definitive link between these attacks and sleep deprivation, drug use, and depression.

The best course of action to take if you suspect you suffer from panic disorder is to speak to a professional therapist as soon as possible. Left unchecked, a panic disorder can spiral totally out of control and result in a paralyzing fear of being outside or confined to small spaces, known as agoraphobia.

Obsessive-compulsive disorder

Obsessive-compulsive disorder (OCD) is classed as a mental disorder that forces the sufferer to repeatedly and spontaneously perform routine tasks or thoughts without much self-control. When these mechanical behaviors like repeatedly washing hands, arranging items in a specific order, or packing and unpacking interfere with your daily routine and social interactions because they become time-consuming, you are very possibly suffering from obsessive-compulsive disorder.

The obsessive-compulsive disorder consists of two very specific disorders, as outlined below:

1. Obsessions are continual, persistent thoughts or impulses over which the sufferer has little control. They usually involve excessive concerns or worries about contamination, symmetry, or forbidden sexual pleasures.

2. Compulsions include repetitive behaviors that a person feels obliged to perform to keep control of their emotions and fill time. Compulsions include uttering repeated phrases or mantras to ward of perceived evils, or constantly cleaning and disinfecting their hands or bodies as well as the areas in which they work and live. Cognitive-behavioral therapy and exposure therapy are often the preferred treatments for obsessive-compulsive disorder (Gorrindo & Parekh, 2017).

Phobias

The word phobia is derived from the Greek word 'Phobos' (horror) and is considered a type of anxiety disorder that creates an excessive, unjustified fear or aversion to an object, a person, or a situation over which you feel you have no control (Wodele & Solan, 2017).

Many different phobias exist, and not all of these are necessarily treatable through professional means unless, of course, they become all-consuming and begin to impact your life negatively.

- ❖ Arachnophobia is the fear of spiders that is perhaps the most common phobia in Western culture.
- ❖ Nyctophobia is an unexplained fear of the dark.

- ❖ Hydrophobia is an aversion to water.

- ❖ Acrophobia is a very real fear of heights or high places.

- ❖ Agoraphobia is a common fear of crowds being in the outdoors.

- ❖ Claustrophobia is the fear of having no escape from being closed into a small space.

Treatment for phobias usually takes the form of psychotherapy or exposure therapy. The therapist takes the patient through a series of exercises that assist in identifying the specific disorder, which can then be addressed. In some mild cases, talking the problem through is sufficient to help you overcome your fear. However, in more severe cases, the solution may come by being exposed, under controlled conditions, to the fear-inducing object or situation in order to successfully address it.

Generalized anxiety disorder

People suffering from generalized anxiety disorder (GAD) worry superabundantly and continuously about a wide variety of things that may include work, money, the weather or their health issues, to name but a few. They often appear to be caught on a 'disaster treadmill,' anticipating calamities and dwelling on all the negative aspects of life. This affliction may affect more women than men and can have far-reaching detrimental effects on relationships, work ethic, successful living, and your overall well-being.

Treatment can take the form of Supportive or Interpersonal Therapies, although cognitive-behavioral therapy can also play a valuable role. Medication can be prescribed in severe cases ("Generalized Anxiety Disorder," n.d.).

Social anxiety disorder

Social anxiety disorder (SAD) is a mental health issue that predominantly manifests as fear of social situations. People suffering from social anxiety disorder prefer not to mix with others and may often live alone as hermits.

If you are afraid of being judged by others and self-conscious and uncomfortable meeting other people, or maybe you feel you are constantly being watched, you may well suffer from Social anxiety disorder. Social anxiety disorder affects many people and creates negative feelings about others as well as themselves. Many sufferers experience what is termed performance disorder. Although these people may feel sufficiently comfortable to mix with others, they become totally uncomfortable, anxious, and withdrawn when expected to take part in proceedings, such as giving a speech or being asked to lead a group in song.

Social anxiety disorder often runs in families and usually begins during the sufferer's youth when they are shy and unsure of themselves. If this affliction goes unnoticed and unaddressed, it can become quite debilitating and embarrassing for the individual and negatively impact their chances of reaching their full potential.

Early detection and treatment with psychotherapy can help the sufferer overcome this affliction and lead a successful, happy, well-balanced life. ("Social Anxiety Disorder," n.d.).

Post-traumatic stress disorder

Post-traumatic stress disorder (PTSD) is a mental condition triggered by an actual horrific and terrifying event, either witnessed or experienced. The symptoms usually include flash-backs, haunting memories, nightmares, and severe, uncontrollable anxiety. Unfortunately, PTSD is on the rise in the world because many more people are being subjected to bombings, murders, high-jackings, war, natural disasters, and personal assault.

In some instances where people have been able to work through their fear, they are able to live almost normal lives. They may suffer occasional flash-backs but are generally able to cope. However, in instances where people who have suffered terrible stress and have not been able to receive the correct professional support, the disorder usually worsens to become an all-consuming, destructive force in their lives. The negative impact of PTSD on their work, personal relationships, and general behavior, negates any happiness or balance in life for these sufferers.

Treatment for PTSD is often long-term and must be consistent to be of any value. As with all therapies, we need to buy into the process in order to enjoy its success.

Chapter 4: Taking Control of Your Emotions

Irrespective of the type of anxiety disorder affecting you, it is imperative that you are brave enough to admit you are struggling, and then seek professional advice. You need to follow this advice diligently in order to manage, if not totally overcome, your anxiety challenges.

Sometimes, we are our own worst enemy. By becoming involved in the wrong situations and allowing ourselves to be caught up in emotional spirals of our own making, we inadvertently set ourselves up for failure.

Emotions are powerful personal feelings, thoughts and behavioral responses to fear or pleasure that is directly linked to our nervous system and therefore governed by our brain. There is no actual cut and dried definition for emotions because each person reacts differently to their feelings and executes their own individual actions in response.

In real terms, when you witness or think of something frightening, your brain reacts immediately and releases adrenaline and cortisol, which are your 'fight or flight' stress hormones. Your reaction will be to either run or stand and fight. Either way, your body goes into an immediate state of stress.

The alternate scenario of seeing someone you love, or receiving an unexpected gift or visit from a special person encourages your brain to release serotonin, dopamine, and oxytocin, which are your happy hormones.

These emotions have been in existence in the human race since time began and are responsible for our survival as a species. In times past, the desire to survive, hunt, procreate stemmed from man's interpretation of simple, straight forward signals about life and death situations.

The modern man struggles to interpret the many confusing signals being sent and received in our modern world. Not only are people unable to communicate clearly and honestly, but we are faced with electronic communication devices that have robbed humanity of face-to-face confrontations. Personal visual clues provided by facial expressions and gestures are no longer utilized. Instead, emojis have to suffice.

Perfection Versus Power

Emotions have a powerful effect on you and determine how successful you are in your relationships as well as in your life in general. By gaining control over your emotions, you will ensure you become mentally stronger and more focused.

In the twenty-first century, humanity is focused primarily on perfection. You are assaulted daily by adverts for the perfect type of hair, for amazingly shaped beautiful bodies, for just the right style of clothing or footwear, for the most seductive vehicle to drive or magnificent home in which to live. Bombarded by all this artificial glamor, it is no wonder you become stressed. Your brain has been trained to see perfection as the only goal in life; anything less is registered as a failure. And failure means anxiety because you are falling short of the benchmark.

You often become caught up in the eternal spiral of searching for continual yet elusive success, and your brain is not always able to tell reality from fiction. As a result, your brain begins to register and emit multiple stress signals throughout the day, some of which are for totally inconsequential reasons.

To regain power over your emotions, you need to focus first on what is real and of true value. Once you learn to make this distinction, you will no longer be slaves to your emotions but rather in total control of what you allow into your mind and ultimately your lives to bring you pleasure, peace, and happiness.

Handling Emotions for Success

Your emotions are closely linked to your own personal inner psyche, which has developed since babyhood. Gradually we learn to interpret the sensations we experience, such as hunger, tiredness, pain, cold, and discomfort and begin to realize there are solutions to each of these sensations. If we are fortunate enough to enjoy the loving support of parents and a family, learning is pleasurable and we develop warm 'fuzzy' feelings that aid us in understanding our emotions. There will, however, be times in our lives when we are unable to communicate the exact emotion we are experiencing, and it is at times such as these that we will generally turn to a secondary source for advice or comfort.

The media exercises a powerful hold over humanity, manipulating us into spending money and purchasing items we do not need, driving our desires for better material possessions, and even forcing us to diet and only eat certain foods. The advertisers ensure their models are always happy, smiling, and promoting the good side of life. The images of perfect people with perfect lifestyles and families, plenty of money and smart cars, creates a false sense of reality.

For the average person who struggles day to day to make a living, this fantasy world promoted by the media is absolutely proven to create huge emotional problems. The American dream is not as easy as it appears. So when you and I become stressed and show any sort of emotion other than the artificial smile, we are coded as emotional, unstable or over-sensitive. The result is that we begin to believe that only good people are beautiful and always happy. The media has forced society to judge us all according to its standard of what it means to be happy. Therefore, if we experience emotions other than happiness, we are abnormal, and emotions other than happiness are unacceptable and should never be shown.

The result? Many people prefer not to show emotion in any form. Managing your emotions successfully is not about ignoring or suppressing them and hoping they will simply disappear. Being human, we all, however, experience a variety of emotions on a daily basis, and so when you cannot or choose not to show these, what do you do with them? You bottle them up, hide them, and pretend they do not exist. And then, when you get to bursting point and explode, you are labeled 'sick' or 'mental.' Your own self-confidence takes a dive as you begin to chastise and criticize yourselves for being weak.

Recognizing your emotions and being able to label them correctly gives you the edge on how best to handle them. Some emotions mask your true feelings, and this can be a dangerous situation because you may then be unable to identify the underlying cause for the emotion you are experiencing. For example, sensations of anger may mask your feelings of insecurity or perhaps even embarrassment. Sometimes you may experience a variety of emotions at the same time, like fear followed closely by anger, then topped off with sadness. Giving your emotions a name enables you to gain power over them.

The Steps to Take to Gain Control of Our Emotions

Emotions have a tendency to run away with us if we don't keep them under control. Understanding who we are and how we react in specific circumstances can be helpful for controlling our emotional responses. For example, if you know that standing in a long queue and watching people 'cut the line' makes your blood boil, save yourself the headache and visit the bank or supermarket earlier in the day to avoid the long wait. Or when your mother-in-law calls, as always, just as you are about to settle the baby for the night, don't let this act add to your stress. Put the phone on silent and call her back later. When we are able to think rationally about what rattles our cages, we are often able to think of a suitable solution, but when we are in the thick of the moment, self-restraint and logic can somehow simply disappear. A number of important steps are suggested for us to follow in order to assist us in improving our emotional management skills.

Step 1: Relearn the facts

Fact One

Different emotions like happiness, anger, and anxiety that make us feel good or bad are normal and should be accepted as such. The quicker we learn to identify which emotion is which, the faster we can adequately respond.

Fact Two

Emotions are feelings we experience as a result of our brain interpreting stimuli received via our senses. For example, information received via the media can be viewed as either a threat or a reward. We know our brain cannot distinguish between fantasy and reality without our own personal input, so it is vital for us to remain in control of our thoughts and be the master of our own destiny. If we correctly identify the stimulus, we can respond, or not, with the appropriate emotion.

Fact Three

Every person is different and will, therefore, experience situations in a slightly different way to other people. Their emotional responses will, therefore, also differ. Some peoples' responses may be more intense, while others are less so.

Fact Four

It is normal for emotions to vary from one set of circumstances to another, and no two responses will ever be identical.

Fact Five

Because humans are complex beings, we are capable of experiencing more than one emotion simultaneously.

Fact Six

We should consistently acknowledge and respond to our emotions; however, they should not always be believed. When we are bombarded daily by perfect icons of humanity, we need to accept these models at face value and realize our chances of being able to emulate them are slim to none. So why worry about the unattainable? Instead, use what you already have to your advantage and make the best success of your life that you can.

Fact Seven

Emotions usually begin in our bodies and because we are so out of touch with our own reality, we often miss the signs of emotion beginning to develop. Unfortunately, by the time we identify these emotions, it is often too late to adequately manage the consequences.

Step 2: Early recognition of emotions is the key to successful management of emotions

Some people find it difficult to identify their emotions and are not always sure of exactly how they are feeling or how they should be feeling in a specific situation. Other people become so totally wrapped up in their emotions that they lose sight of reality and experience feelings of being trapped.

In order for us to regain control over our emotions and keep them in check, we need to understand each emotion and be able to accurately interpret it.

Body scan

Regularly throughout your day, make an effort to reconnect with your body and do a 'body scan'. Close your eyes and starting at your toes, slowly envisage each body part and take note of any physical sensations it is emitting. So for example, if you are feeling sad, instead of focusing on the sadness, try to experience how your body is feeling: My heart is aching; I have a lump in my throat; my eyes are teary. Once you are able to identify your body's reactions to specific emotions, you will be able to avoid situations that cause these emotions.

Journal magic

Try keeping a journal of your emotional responses to specific situations. The process of writing gives you the opportunity to express your emotions in words. This, in itself, can prove quite therapeutic.

Emotion check

Learn as much as you can about different emotions and how these emotions make you feel. Our brain interprets stimuli collected through our senses, and depending on the type of information received, it will produce the correct hormones accordingly. Often throughout our day, we are faced with a variety of situations that make us anxious. The brain produces the necessary hormones to keep us in 'fight or flight' mode. Our bodies remain tense, muscles tight and ready for action. Our heart rate increases along with our breathing. This tense state may continue on and off throughout the day, leaving us in a state of panic or experiencing an anxiety attack. Because our brain cannot distinguish between what is really dangerous and what is not, it is up to us to consciously take control of the situation and calm down.

Hold on to reality

In every stressful situation, it is important not to lose sight of reality. Try to develop ways to 'self-soothe' and restore balance and harmony to your life. This may involve deep breathing exercises or relaxation techniques. Go with whatever 'floats your boat'. Re-centering yourself regularly during the day will ensure that you give your body ample opportunity to restore itself and to avoid unnecessary 'blow-ups'.

Emotions are transitory

Keep in mind that emotions are normal experiences and transitory. They will come and go and be replaced by other emotions as you are faced with different situations. The secret is to be able to recognize situations that give rise to a specific emotion and where possible (although not always practical) acknowledge the feeling and then let it go. To hold onto your emotions is like carrying an increasingly heavy shopping bag on your shoulder that creates unnecessary stress. Empty the 'bag' regularly and stay sane!

Mindfulness magic

Mindfulness has become a buzz word in the Western world and is one of the possible solutions to dealing with modern-day stress and anxiety disorders. It is believed to have its roots in Buddhist meditation.

Mindfulness is a simple term for a rather complex process. The word means being in tune with yourself and maintaining a close and caring awareness of your own feelings, sensations, and thoughts.

Practicing mindfulness and meditation has shown benefits for the restoration of your sense of well-being and inner peace, as well as helping to re-balance and re-energize yourself. Mindfulness creates a sense of inner calm, which is beneficial to improving sleep patterns and boosting your immune system. It increases your positive thoughts, improves your memory, and increases your attention span and enables you to recall facts and information with improved accuracy.

Mindfulness training may improve our empathy and assist us in more readily identifying people in need of support. It is known to play a vital, positive role in relationships by increasing mutual awareness and care as well as improving intimacy.

Mindful people have an elevated self-esteem, a healthier body-image, and they generally act more in line with ethical values and morals.

Mindfulness increases our resilience and makes us better able to combat illness.

Mindful people show fewer instances of bias or prejudice and have a more balanced outlook on life. Mindfulness training could be successful for managers, parents, students, and teachers, because it lays the perfect foundation for creativity, positive thinking, self-confidence as well as self-control.

All in all, mindfulness training may be the single most valuable tool you will ever need to decrease your stress and get your life back on track. Although mindfulness training sounds like a panacea for all ills, it requires commitment and diligent practice to see results.

The big sleep

Rest is vital for life, but the value of good, regular, healthy sleep routines can never be underestimated. Anxiety and depression are aggravated by lack of sleep. Ensure you enjoy sufficient good quality sleep. A tired body and mind cannot function at their optimum.

Professional support

Do not hesitate to seek professional support to help you understand your emotions and for advice on how best to keep them in check. By paying careful attention to these important skills, we will learn more about our emotions and how to handle them in order to prevent moments of madness and the onset of depression and to create and maintain balance in our lives.

Chapter 5: Emotional Intelligence and Empathy

Emotionally intelligent individuals generally demonstrate a clear understanding and awareness of their emotions. They confidently exercise control over these sentiments and express them in meaningful ways in order to successfully manage interpersonal relationships with empathy and understanding. They are capable of successfully processing emotions and being able to make a sound judgment based on emotional evidence.

Emotional intelligence is a hypothesis that was used during the 1980s and '90s in an attempt to rationalize the illogical and sometimes erratic behavior of highly intelligent people. In instances where exceptionally intelligent individuals behave in a bizarre and irrational manner, they are accorded a low EQ.

An example of someone with a high IQ but a low EQ might be the fanatical scientist who wears the same baggy, food be speckled jacket every day and doesn't see the need to brush his matted hair. On the other hand, you may meet an uneducated street hustler with a low IQ and a high EQ, who may easily con you into parting with your money.

A person's IQ is a relatively stable objective measurement of their general intelligence that is not likely to change and is, therefore, easier to quantify. On the other hand, however, emotional intelligence (EQ) is subjective and by its very nature variable, and is, therefore, more difficult to measure. (Cherry, 2019).

Skills to Help You Develop Emotional Intelligence

So, no matter how smart you are or how high your IQ might be, you need to work on developing your EQ if you want to live a successful, well-balanced, happy life. Here are some ideas to help you develop a smarter EQ.

Practice self-awareness

This is perhaps the most challenging process to begin with because if you don't take control of your emotions, they sure will take control of you! So start by becoming self-aware. Practicing self-awareness means understanding who you really are and why you behave as you do. There are three important components to consider here:

❖ Know what you are actually doing

❖ Understand how your actions make you feel

❖ Acknowledge your inner emotional state

Knowing what you are actually doing

Let's begin by exploring the concept of knowing exactly what you are doing. Are you grounded and aware of every activity in which you participate during your day? Probably not. Because most people in the twenty-first century are so bogged down with repetitive trivial matters like texting, emailing, and maybe watching YouTube, that they have lost sight of the real tasks that actually matter. These involve communicating face-to-face with your partner and children, stopping by a neighbor to inquire about their health, chatting and smiling with the local store owner, or taking your dogs for a walk.

To successfully identify what you are busy with, you need to get rid of distractions like your cellphone, television, any drugs or alcohol, housework, or work and just examine yourself without these appendages. These distractions fill our time and 'protect' us from facing reality and acknowledging failure, loneliness, and fear.

If you are able to set aside a specific amount of time, say about 10 minutes each day, to just contemplate who you are and what you are achieving in life, you will soon realize you need to change direction if you want to be happy and successful.

Understanding how your actions make you feel

So now you have shelved all the distractions for a period, how do you feel? This is quite a frightening question because many people find it difficult to express how they feel. The whirlwind of life carries us forward, and we are seldom given a chance to examine our true feelings amidst the rush and bustle of life.

You may find you are shocked by the sensations of sadness, loneliness, anger, or frustration that suddenly crowd your psyche. How do you cope with these overwhelming sensations? Most of us go back to what we were doing before, filling our lives with distractions so that we don't ever have to face the truth about how we really feel.

Ask yourself if your work brings you satisfaction, or is it purely a way to earn money to feed and house your family? Do you feel joy and contentment when you spend time with your loved ones? Or are you anxious and afraid or feeling depressed and unsure about your future?

Scary though this may be, you need to discover how your actions really make you feel in order for you to make decisions about whether you continue in the same path or change direction completely. It sounds like a 'survive or die' scenario, and maybe it is?

Acknowledge your inner emotional state

If you have reached this step, you are well on your way to making good progress in getting to know your true self and learning to be more self-aware.

So, now you have to identify all the emotions that have surfaced during your time of self-contemplation. You also need to decide why you are experiencing these particular feelings. Maybe you feel angry all the time because you believe people don't accord you the respect you feel is due. Perhaps you experience great loneliness or sadness and depression because you are unable to mix comfortably with people due to your low self-esteem.

Once you have acknowledged your emotions, you can set about improving the way in which you handle situations. Create more calmness and serenity in your life. Be kinder to yourself first and then find ways to treat others better. Gradually as you practice self-awareness, you will develop empathy, a deep understanding of yourself as well as your fellow men.

From self-awareness grows inner peace and the ability to see life in perspective. So try not to 'sweat-the-small-stuff' that makes you anxious and crabby. Practice viewing the bigger picture called 'life' and enjoy living it to the fullest.

Channel your emotions carefully

Your emotions are fluid and constantly on the move. They are a series of endless signals you receive every second of the day that demand your attention to specific incidents and actions in the world around us.

Depending on how you respond to your emotions will influence your life in either a positive or negative manner. Emotions cannot be simply classified as 'good' or 'bad,' but your reaction to these emotions can. If you experience anger and direct your actions towards others with the intent to harm them, your reaction to the anger you are feeling is bad. If, however, you direct your actions towards others in order to protect your loved ones from harm, then your reaction to your anger is good.

The importance of channeling your response to your emotions cannot be underestimated. Recognizing your emotions and being able to decide on the correct course of action to take is the ultimate goal for achieving emotional intelligence.

An emotionally intelligent person does not waste time and energy focusing on the negative emotions and reactions rather than by manipulating the good emotions to their own benefit.

Learn self-motivation techniques

Self-motivation is an important aspect of any individual's success. You cannot expect motivation to just develop without some effort on your part. Once you decide to improve your emotional intelligence, you have taken the first step towards self-motivation. So by the simple activity to 'taking action,' you are, in fact, promoting motivation.

Don't let procrastination steal your valuable time, because thinking about doing something without actually making a start robs us of the opportunity to complete tasks within a specified time frame.

Focus on the positive aspects of completing a task by telling yourself how satisfied you feel when the job is done. This will elicit positive emotions that will act as an encouragement for you.

Mindfulness is a valuable tool for developing useful self-motivation techniques. It trains your brain to focus on the positive aspects of your life, and by breathing deeply in a controlled manner, you are able to dissolve anxiety and visualize yourself in a healthy space. Through mindfulness training, you can learn to live within your given space in the present while remaining alert and consciously aware of your surroundings. You will be motivated to develop a more positive mindset that will stand you in good stead for solving future difficulties.

Emotional intelligence supports healthier relationships

Any relationship begins with the recognition of and respect for the emotions of the people involved.

The whole idea of improving our emotional intelligence is to ultimately be in a prime position to grow and develop our personal romantic, familial and social relationships. People with emotional intelligence are better able to foster healthy relationships with others.

In order to develop successful relationships, you need to associate with other individuals and demonstrate your care, interest, and empathy in them.

Caring for others involves stepping out of your own comfort zone and extending your hand in support or friendship (or both) to another human being. This is not always an easy task due to the fact that modern people live largely insular lives and don't often encourage sincere, caring contact with their fellow men.

Showing a real interest in other people is also a challenge in modern times. Each individual may be desperate to connect with another but may feel too insecure to make a move for fear of being rebuffed.

And finally, empathy involves accepting other people for who they are without actually needing to fully understand them. When you truly empathize with someone, you are able to experience and rejoice in their happiness, or ache and commiserate when they suffer, as if these emotions were your very own. Understanding the value of empathy helps us realize we are an integral part of something much greater and more complex than we may at first have imagined.

Without making the effort to truly connect with others, there is little chance for building successful, lasting and happy relationships with anyone. Through developing good relationships, we add value to our lives, and our values define who we really are. Flood your emotions with positive values (Shatto, 2018).

The true importance of acquiring emotional intelligence is to use it for the good of others and not manipulate or abuse them in any way. Genuine empathy aims at being beneficial to everyone. How can we ensure this process is successful? We learn to place value on people by treating them with respect and acknowledging and appreciating their individuality.

By uplifting others instead of manipulating them for our personal gain, we offer them the opportunity to realize that our values govern our actions. When we are able to recognize the value of our actions as generous and charitable, we can admit that we have achieved emotional intelligence.

Chapter 6: Emotional Literacy and Business Success

Emotional intelligence is perhaps the most critical gauge for success in relationships because it is not only the savvy to recognize and identify your own emotions but those of others as well. Since relationships form the basic cornerstone for every aspect of our lives, it is little wonder that emotional intelligence is of huge value to your business success.

Successful Performance in the Workplace

High performance in the workplace is closely linked to high emotional intelligence. Sadly, however, many managers have low to no emotional intelligence. They gained power and prestige through their high general intelligence (IQ) but are, in fact, not at all suitable for managerial positions because of their lack of empathy and ability to interact positively with their employees.

Manage your own negative emotions

The secret to understanding others is first to ensure your view of them is not distorted in any way by your own negative emotions. It is not an easy task to work with a variety of different personalities, each with their own set of personal circumstances and peculiar hang-ups.

Practice mindfulness when dealing with people. Study each individual closely and recognize their emotional responses to everyday work issues. Once you have established how they are reacting to situations, you can begin to discover the 'why? In this way, you are less likely to become upset by your employees but rather more tolerant and understanding. You will, therefore, be better at managing these people, and they may well be more responsive.

Be mindful of your vocabulary

Improved communication skills are a sure way to positively influence the people with whom you work. Emotionally intelligent managers are able to use specific types of questions to elicit the responses they need from their employees. They are capable of pinpointing specific problems quickly and with minimum stress and are then generally able to suggest suitable resolutions.

Practice empathy

A good manager will pay attention to the verbal as well as non-verbal clues of his employees in order to ascertain their true feelings and emotions. Try to imagine walking in your employee's shoes' and be mindful of the issues they may have to face daily. Showing empathy does not mean that you are willing to condone irresponsible, unacceptable behavior. It does, however, give you the 'heads-up' on the possible reasons for this behavior and affords you the opportunity to assist your employees in managing it successfully.

Recognize what 'presses your buttons'

Knowledge of what behaviors and actions cause you to go into a total spiral can assist you in pre-empting this response by removing these catalysts or learning to deal with them in an emotionally intelligent manner. So, if having an employee barge through your door first thing in the morning (before you have even had the chance to pull out your chair) really sets you off, lock the door for the first half-hour or so of your day to give yourself the chance to settle into your own routine.

Bounce back in a positive manner

Adversity and frustration are part of life. The way in which you deal with these daily frustrations, however, will depend on your level of emotional intelligence. This is not to say that you should become insensitive or treat adversity lightly. Rather learn to demonstrate a positive response to calamity and instead of having a 'melt-down' practice optimism. Ask yourself how this situation could have been avoided and take confident steps towards resolving it.

Emotional intelligence is not a static commodity but rather a skill that can grow and improve over time. A good, emotionally intelligent manager is aware of this fact and will ensure this process of development is on-going.

The Importance of Empathy

The definition of empathy

Empathy is a much valued but little owned skill. Some people have a natural tendency to have empathy, while for others, it is a skill to be learned. Empathy involves the physical, innate ability an individual has to sense and understand the emotions felt by another person and to be able to respond appropriately.

The value empathy has for any relationship, whether it be of a personal, social or work-related nature, cannot be underestimated.

The categories of empathy

Empathy can be categorized in one of two ways. Firstly it can be termed 'affective empathy,' which refers specifically to the sensations you experience when you witness another person's distress or happiness. Your brain mirrors those emotions and releases memories of similar experiences in your life. This process allows you to be able to commiserate or rejoice as required.

The second interpretation of empathy is that of 'cognitive empathy,' which relates directly to the cognitive function of being able to interpret and understand another person's emotional state in terms of what you already know about similar emotions. Interestingly, people on the autistic spectrum seldom exercise cognitive empathy because of their limited understanding and experience with identifying and expressing emotions.

The history of empathy

Empathy appears to have its core in your unfolding history, and elementary forms have been noted in primates and even in dogs and rats. Associated with two different brain pathways activated by 'mirror neurons' that assist your brain in recalling an image and playing this back in your memory in a mirror-like fashion when you witness a similar action performed by someone else. Your brain recalls not only the 'picture' but also the sensations associated with the image. Your empathetic reaction puts you straight into the other person's shoes, so to speak and you identify immediately with their emotions.

Empathy and Compassion

Empathy and compassion are often linked due to the fact that they are both positive emotions generally aimed at supporting and offering solace to others in need. When you take notice of someone who is disadvantaged or suffering in some way, you take cognizance of their circumstances. Once you recognize their plight, you are in a good position to show compassion, tender concern, and consideration.

Empathy is understanding, by virtue of your own previous similar experiences, how the person is feeling; while compassion is your willingness to intervene and offer support.

The Role of Empathy in Our Lives

As previously stated, empathy, although an integral and vital component in your life, is seldom acknowledged and is practiced by only a few people. It involves being capable of understanding something from the perspective of someone else. This simply means you can share their feelings and understand their emotions because they resonate with you personally. The outcome of this understanding is that you are able to demonstrate compassion to the people, not only in your family and at your place of work, but in society in general.

Compassion drives your actions to be kind and helpful, to show courtesy and care to people. It encourages you to assist that elderly person to cross the street, or to pick up the fallen items for a person whose shopping bag has disintegrated. Compassion produces unselfish, random acts of kindness and support without any desire for compensation.

Empathy and compassion work hand in hand. There are many instances in which their partnership plays a vital role.

In your personal life

Empathy and compassion are essential players in love relationships and marriage. Healthy relationships need to be nurtured with care if they are to continue to grow and reap the rewards of longevity, successful companionship, deep understanding, and lasting love.

In your place of work

Your workplace is the allocated area where teamwork and the co-operative effort are required for the successful completion of specific tasks. In order for projects to be accomplished, it is imperative for all team members to understand each other, acknowledge each other's strengths and weaknesses and offer each member the support needed to get the job done. Showing empathy to your fellow team players enables you to understand their frustrations and concerns about the job. A good manager will use empathy to garner the support of his employees for the benefit of the company.

In the world at large

Showing empathy to those around you in your daily life gives you an edge over other people who have not yet mastered the skill. Your popularity is sure to improve as you become more caring and demonstrate compassion for those you meet. The smile you give the lady at the checkout counter, the cheerful wave to the kids who pass by on the school bus, the warm, sincere greeting you give your family at the end of your busy day say a lot about who you really are. People generally respond positively to your confident, upbeat approach, and their acknowledgment boosts your self-esteem.

Humanity appears to be caught in a state of limbo, governed by the power of electronic devices and reluctant to become involved in anything requiring the commitment of self. Empathy and compassion have a way of multiplying when they are shared. It's like the concept of passing on a good deed. The world needs more compassionate, caring people to help it re-energize its dormant desire for interpersonal connections.

How to Develop Empathy

Empathy is a skill you have acquired from birth through mimicking parental examples, or you have learned during your lifetime of interacting with other people in a positive and constructive manner. It is closely linked to compassion and emotional intelligence, both of which can often be learned in the home.

It is, however, unfortunately, not a widely practiced skill and should perhaps be added to the school curriculum as a compulsory subject for study.

Developing empathy is worth all the effort it takes. The long-term positive effects of acting with empathy and compassion have already been mentioned.

Here are some suggestions of ways in which you can develop empathy in your home:

Train your children

Early training of your children to share toys and equipment, to wait their turn with patience, to show respect for their seniors, to be mindful of the needs of those who are less fortunate, to play by the rules of the game, and to not always have to be a winner will kick start their empathy skills from a young age.

Train yourself

You can train yourself by reading and studying the abundant material available on the subject. Also, practice this learned empathy at every opportunity. You may well be amazed at the responses you get and the progress you see.

Listen with patience

Listen to other people, including your partner and your children, with patience and respect. Show an interest in what they are saying and answer them accordingly. Good communication skills involve not only speaking but also listening.

Recognize effort

Many people appreciate recognition for their efforts. This holds true for your home environment as well as your place of work. If you are a manager or a parent, try to step back for a moment and allow someone else the opportunity to be noticed and applauded.

Reject stereotyping

Reject stereotyping and teach children to accept their peers even if they are different in some way. Maybe there is a child in a wheelchair or someone who wears spectacles in your child's class. Navigate these situations ethically and with compassion while you encourage your children to accept their peers with genuine enthusiasm. Together you can welcome a child new to the country into your neighborhood and model to your children how to be patient as this child learns the new language.

Examples of How Empathy Works in Your Life

At school

Empathy is an integral factor in being a helpful, meaningful, and responsible member of your school community. Learners who demonstrate empathy seldom become involved in altercations at school and do not bully their peers.

Good academic grades and career success can be attributed to learners with empathy skills who are able to work cooperatively and with good team spirit. Schools where empathy and compassion are fostered, are peaceful, productive places where positive learning is promoted.

Although teaching empathy takes consistent commitment and time, the rewards are well worth the effort. Children and young people demonstrate a natural capacity for empathy and although they may not have been exposed to it prior to school. Once the skills have been learned, there is usually an improvement in classroom management and noticeably higher academic achievement and better communication skills. Practicing empathy reduces incidents of bullying and results in fewer aggressive outbursts and behavioral disorders.

In your place of work

Your interaction with your work colleagues should give a clear indication of your respect for them. It may not always be easy to work cooperatively with every member of the team. But, if you are capable of listening attentively to people and you make an effort to understand what makes them tick, you are more likely to enjoy a successful working career.

Your interpersonal skills say a lot about who you really are, and if your skills are good, your chance of successfully leading a team is pretty high.

You may wish to consider these three simple ways to improve your empathy at work:

Listen with interest

To develop the skills to really listen with a genuine interest in what someone is saying affords you the opportunity to study their body language as well and to better understand the message they are trying to communicate.

Many people can hear a wide variety of sounds with which we are bombarded on a daily basis, but how many actually 'tune in' to listen when someone speaks? Listening is a learned skill which, if successfully accomplished, requires the listener to be fully aware of not only the sounds and syllables being made but also the nuances in the speech pattern as well as the facial expression of the speaker. Using all these clues, the listener can gain valuable insight into the speaker as well as better understand their message.

Show respect

Respect is a learned behavior, and if taught correctly in the home will stand you in good stead in all future interpersonal relationships. Whether you are a manager or one of the employees, showing respect is a sure way to garner a reciprocal reaction.

Greet your colleagues with warmth and show appreciation for what they are doing. Take time to find out a bit about their personal lives and families. Although some people prefer not to disclose personal information in the workplace, they may appreciate your interest and value your concern.

Step out of your comfort zone

Make an attempt to visualize yourself in your colleagues' position and ask yourself how this may make you feel. As soon as you realize their anxiety or trepidation at taking on new tasks, you are better able to offer support and advice. Stand back from situations and try to remain objective in your assessment of someone. Don't allow your emotions to cloud your judgment but rather attempt to judge their actions on merit.

Barriers to Empathy

Much has been said about the importance of empathy in every area of our lives. However, to recap, barriers to empathy are surreptitious and can be affected by your own prejudice and insecurity. Keeping a watchful eye out for any of the following barriers will enable you to protect your empathy from being needlessly destroyed.

Intolerance and prejudice

Prejudice and intolerance go hand-in-hand and are two of the biggest barriers to empathy. Acceptance of people for who they are is easier said than done. Some personalities are more likable than others.

However, when you show true empathy you have the ability to put aside any prejudice or preconceived ideas about the people with whom you work.

Lack of compassion

Compassion is an emotion people tend to lose as they age and become more bogged down by life's challenges. It is, however, a valuable tool in any personal relationship, whether this is fleeting, superficial, or a deep, lasting kind. Lack of compassion robs us of our ability to care about others.

Stacking the deck

When people are aware that the hierarchy in the workplace benefits only those in power, they may quickly lose their sense of commitment to their employer. Although every place of work requires managers and people in control, it's vital for workers to feel part of the team.

Impatience

Treating people in an impatient manner does nothing to create harmony in the workplace. Understanding that everyone has responsibilities and accepting the importance of interacting with your fellow worker for the good of the entire team, goes a long way to creating good work relationships. Patience is a learned skill and although we may expect people to demonstrate it more often, it is only by setting the example that they will have the opportunity to follow.

Selfishness and narcissistic behavior

People who are intrinsically selfish as well as those who display an inflated opinion of themselves and who crave constant attention certainly don't have empathy. Empathy presupposes a willingness to share and to be connected to others.

Avoid assumptions

Everyone is different and unique in their own right. Someone with empathy is not likely to make assumptions about a person on the basis of race, gender, or creed. They will accept the individual for who they are and afford them the opportunity to prove their own worth.

Support

When you show a lack of support for family, friends, and colleagues, you indicate a distinct lack of empathy. Supporting people by listening to them and making an effort to understand their point of view entrenches feelings of acceptance and self-worth.

Guarding against barriers to empathy is not an easy task, but one well worth the effort. The more we all practice our empathy skills, the better life will be.

Chapter 7: Emotional Illiteracy and Relationships

Verbal literacy involves the ability to recognize, read, and understand the written word and those individuals who do not possess these skills are termed illiterate. Another type of illiteracy exists when individuals demonstrate an inability to recognize and understand both their own emotions as well as those of others. These people are then said to suffer from emotional illiteracy.

Unfortunately, many people suffer from emotional illiteracy, which negatively impacts every area of their lives. No matter how smart people are or how high their IQ, if they suffer from low emotional processing skills, they may experience difficulty functioning optimally in their place of work or may find it too challenging to hold down social and intimate relationships.

Being human presupposes an ability to interact socially and emotionally with others of our species. However, many people experience difficulty cooperating with others in an intimate, face-to-face way. Most humans in the twenty-first century are so 'brainwashed' and programed by technological devices to function as loners, that they have lost the ability to spontaneously communicate with other people. The less people interact with each other, the more emotionally illiterate they all become, and the greater the negative impact on their relationships.

Emotionally illiterate people are intrinsically selfish, thinking only of their own needs and desires. Leaders who suffer from this affliction tend to be manipulative, impulsive bullies who use their emotional outbursts to control the masses. They instill fear and anguish in their people and are unable to lead without throwing regular tantrums. Idi Amin is a good example of an individual who suffered from emotional illiteracy.

The Characteristics of Emotional Illiteracy

Emotional illiteracy can be defined by the following:

An inability to manage your own emotions

People suffering from emotional illiteracy have difficulty recognizing their own emotions and implementing these in the correct scenario. They often overreact to situations that, in many cases, would be viewed as minor and may become suddenly and unexpectedly violent.

Their display of emotions is usually inappropriate for the incident or circumstances. For example, someone may inadvertently bump into an individual with low emotional intelligence whose reaction may be to use profanities and punch the offending person.

An inability to recognize and understand other people's emotions

Emotionally illiterate people cannot recognize and often fail to correctly interpret other people's emotions. As an example, a homeless beggar suffering from emotional illiteracy may continue to approach a person for a hand-out even though that individual has already frowned at him in annoyance. The beggar cannot recognize the irritation shown in this scenario.

An inability to exercise self-control

Because people suffering from emotional illiteracy are extra sensitive, they often exhibit a lack of self-control when faced with situations in which they feel they have been victimized or belittled in some way. For example, if someone pushes into a queue in front of an emotionally illiterate individual, there is very likely going to be an unpleasant, explosive reaction.

An inability to empathize with others

Due to their selfish nature, emotionally illiterate people cannot see other people's points of view or understand how others may feel in certain circumstances. This inability to recognize another person's pain or their discomfit makes emotionally illiterate people rather unpopular.

An inability to be flexible

Emotionally illiterate people generally demonstrate inflexible social skills and are often assertive and pedantic. They seldom consider other points of view because of their intrinsic selfish outlook on life and their almost obsessive need to be right and remain unchallenged.

The Value of Teaching Emotional Intelligence

Emotional intelligence is not something we are automatically born with. It is a skill we learn from our parents as well as through our interaction within our society. If our source of information lacks knowledge about and insight into emotional intelligence, there is no way that we can acquire these valuable skills on our own. Many of us reach adulthood suffering from feelings of insecurity and lack of self-worth, and because we lack the correct tools for the task of recognizing and interpreting our own as well as other's emotions, we become good candidates for emotional illiteracy. In order to teach the concept of emotional intelligence, our parents and teachers need to be adequately educated in this field.

The Importance of Good Family Values

Children learn from an early age by mimicking the examples set by their parents. The actions, words, and skills taught during these formative years are imprinted in their receptive brains. It is vitally important for parents to take ownership of their responsibilities to their children. These do not end with housing, feeding, and clothing your offspring. No, indeed, there is a lot more to parenting than may at first meet the eye. Early learning through this process of mimicking can be referred to in simple terms and without disrespect as 'monkey-see-monkey-do,' and when good skills are learned, good behaviors ensue. The onus is, therefore, on the parents and primary caregivers to ensure they set the best examples they can for their children to follow.

The Impact Emotional Illiteracy Has on the Family

A caring, supportive and loving family has as some of its basic tenets, fostering good communication skills, accepting each family member with their 'warts and all.' It also provides a solid platform for optimum learning important life skills such as sharing, teamwork, and developing empathy towards all family members.

In a well-balanced family, emotional literacy is high on the agenda as parents value its importance for the overall successful operation of the family unit. Parents teach their children good listening skills by listening attentively to their and taking a keen interest in what they have to say. Good quality family time is also encouraged and may occur on a daily basis around the dinner table in the evening. Each family member is made to feel welcome, wanted, and special in their own right. Individual skills and talents are encouraged, and efforts are acknowledged and praised. Self-respect, as well as respect for the family, is entrenched by virtue of the example set by the parents. Good family relationships form the basis for future relationships. Problem-solving skills are taught by sharing and discussing problems in a democratic manner. A well-balanced family lives according to a set of well-defined rules which set the boundaries for their understanding of how to work cooperatively within social confines. Children from well-balanced families are known to have a better academic record and are more likely to lead successful lives.

In families where these values are neither acknowledged nor taught, there is little chance of the children learning empathy. Often these families are considered dysfunctional because of the lack of rules and respect, the aggressive attitudes, bad behavior of members of the family towards each other, and the inability for these members to work together for the good of the family. Children from dysfunctional families have fewer advantages at school as well as socially. In rare cases, some have been known to turn their lives around. Most of these have done so when they have realized the importance that empathy plays in developing successful relationships.

Anxiety and Depression Disorders in Emotionally Illiterate Families

The members of dysfunctional families are more likely to suffer from depression and anxiety, although these disorders are not entirely limited to these types of families. Without familial support and acceptance, children from dysfunctional families often have no social 'ground rules' that govern adequate, acceptable behavior. In some instances, a number of these children have the advantage of a caring, empathetic educator who acts as a role model.

Children from dysfunctional families are often at a disadvantage because of their lack of empathy and understanding of the social signals in a group. They are sometimes aggressive and disrespectful of authority, refusing to obey rules and live by socially accepted norms.

Many turn to drugs or alcohol for comfort as none is forthcoming from their family and end up dropping out of school early.

Interestingly enough, a minority of children from well-balanced families sometimes fall prey to bad behavior, illegal substance abuse, and school dropouts. These incidents may be attributed to there being too much 'free cash' available or the influence of bad friends. These children also suffer from anxiety and depression due partly to the pressure under which some parents put them, or their own desire to be the best achiever.

Chapter 8: Emotional Intelligence and Personal Relationships

Emotional intelligence is the key to enduring relationships because it makes us cognizant of the constant changes in ourselves as well as our partner. Life is not static. It is in a constant flexible, fluctuating state, and we, therefore, grow and change accordingly. It is only through acknowledging this process of adaptation and adjustment that we are able to recognize the process in ourselves as well as in our loved ones. An emotionally intelligent individual will make allowances for these changes and 'move with the times' so to speak.

The importance of developing emotional intelligence in your love relationships is that this valuable tool can strengthen your partnerships and help you stay connected while also increasing intimacy and building a love that will stay the course of time (Manson, 2019).

The Impact of Emotional Intelligence on Relationships

Emotional intelligence is perhaps the most important aspect in the development of a close relationship largely because it makes both partners aware of each and every change, large or small, that occurs in themselves and each other. Through this development of active emotional intelligence and intimate sensitivity, both partners will become aware of the nuances and shifts in their relationship that signal the need for a specific action or supportive word or gesture. Emotional intelligence gives rise to the development of empathy, which in turn affords us the opportunity to enjoy a deep and meaningful relationship filled with understanding, mutual caring and support, and the ability to share and enjoy a mutually beneficial emotional relationship. Wow! Wouldn't we all just love to be able to enjoy such bliss? Well, we can, but it takes effort and commitment. One hundred percent from each partner, to be exact, but it is possible only when we realize the value of growing and developing our own emotional intelligence.

In most relationships, trust, honesty, integrity, and the ability to communicate are viewed as being very important elements. And indeed these are. However, another factor, perhaps the most important one, that supersedes all others, is that of emotional intelligence. Why is this so? Mainly because emotional intelligence enables individuals in a relationship to recognize, adequately express, and manage their emotions in a positive way. This is particularly important when difficult emotions arise.

While some people appear to have been naturally gifted with being emotionally intelligent, others may need to learn this extremely valuable skill. Either way, emotional intelligence has long-term benefits for the success of your relationships.

Building Emotionally Intelligent Romantic Relationships

A sharp, alert emotional awareness will guide us towards finding the best romantic partner instead of falling prey to lustful relationships that end up being like a flash-in-the-pan, both harmful and short-lived.

Why settle for the conflict that develops between two people who want their own needs met at the cost of their partner, or resign ourselves to living a life filled with bickering and discontent when we can live life to the full by developing and exercising our emotional intelligence?

The value of high emotional intelligence

High emotional intelligence will support our choice of a good partner and protect us by:

- ❖ Helping us to avoid believing infatuation is the precursor to a lasting relationship
- ❖ Encouraging us to deal with discontent and negative emotions quickly and effectively in order to avoid these festering and ultimately demolishing the relationship
- ❖ Keeping us vigilant to the positive as well as negative aspects of life that can either grow or destroy our relationship

People with well developed emotional intelligence acknowledge and allow, and in fact, encourage, applaud and support their partners' growth and change. They view this process as beneficial to both their individual growth as well as their relationship because their love continues to grow and become more intimate and passionate over time, and is, therefore, more fulfilling.

Developing a great relationship with your partner

Developing a well-balanced, loving relationship with your partner is vital to growing and sustaining the relationship. So how do we get started on growing this much sought after type of relationship with our partner?

Actively seek to change your relationship

Most people are afraid of change because they fear the unknown. However, change can be positive and the start of a whole new and wonderful partnership. Relationships are not static encapsulated entities, but rather dynamic, interactive, vibrant dimensions of our lives.

To change something takes courage and courage, in turn, requires optimism and faith in the possibility of achieving success. Like with all life, care and attention promotes growth and blossoming and will eventually lead to the production of good, wholesome fruit. Without making a concerted effort to improve your relationship, there can be no growth or development. Once a relationship begins to stagnate, the chance of reviving it declines dramatically.

External influences can have a devastating impact on any relationship, no matter how strong it may be. Without the partners being emotionally intelligent, the chances of them even noticing the signs of the potential breakdown in their relationship, let alone seeking to repair and rebuild it, are minimum.

Relationships are a two-way street that automatically assumes communication and interaction. For a relationship to be successful, it stands to reason that both participants should be willing and enthusiastic to interact together in a positive manner.

View the challenges you face as opportunities for growth

Apportioning blame in a failed relationship is one of the most destructive elements that partners can use. As stated previously, life is not a static process, and therefore change and growth should be welcomed and encouraged. Change, by its very nature, brings new dimensions to the relationship, which can be a daunting prospect. If both partners have a positive outlook on the relationship and exercise their emotional intelligence, they will welcome change and view it as an opportunity to grow their relationship to the 'next level.'

When you have a high emotional intelligence, you are able to avoid blaming your partner, and you are seldom hesitant to recognize negative emotions and deal with them immediately in order that they no longer have power over your relationship. In fact, emotionally intelligent people make good use of negative situations to develop positive results and use these to strengthen their relationship, through a deeper understanding of their partner and by drawing closer to each other and becoming more intimate.

Respect each other's feelings

It is important to remember that each person is an individual in their own right. No two people are alike in every way, not even identical twins. Although some character traits in your partner may not delight you, you need to learn to accept your partner, warts and all and to love them unconditionally. With empathy, this is possible. This does not, however, mean that you will never feel anger, frustration, disappointment, or even jealousy. It does mean that you will be able to experience all these emotions, identify them for what they are, deal with them in a positive and constructive manner, and move on with growing your relationship. A tall order for some of us, but by growing and developing our emotional intelligence, not an impossible one.

Maintain humor in your relationships

Having a sense of humor is of great value in every aspect of your life. Being able to laugh at yourself first and foremost is important. This does not mean that you belittle yourself or others, but rather acknowledge your foibles and flaws without taking them too seriously. None of us is perfect. If we were, life would be pretty boring. It's the interesting characteristics in people that attract us to each other in the first place.

Laughter helps us to accept and be tolerant of imperfections in ourselves and others and to encourage us to rise above the unrealistic expectations of being perfect.

Pay attention to how you feel when you are alone

Can you tolerate time away from your loved one? Many people will probably attest to feelings of loneliness, insecurity, restlessness, and possibly resentment when they are separated from their partner. These emotions can have a detrimental effect on any relationship if they are allowed to increase and become unmanageable. However, if you have a well-developed emotional intelligence, you are more likely to view periods of separation from your loved one as opportunities to plan new and exciting ventures to share together.

Show empathy to your loved one

Showing your partner that you are able to put their needs before your own and prioritize understanding their feelings before your own is a sign of being emotionally intelligent. This does not mean that you should become a 'doormat' and always take second place in the relationship. It simply means you are open to paying attention to your partner's needs and you are able to successfully communicate with each other in a positive and fulfilling manner.

Be 'love smart'

"Love smart' appears to have a number of possible meanings. The best one for this topic on emotional intelligence refers to your ability to make good love choices based on your sound knowledge of how to recognize and interpret other people's emotions as well as your own. When you exercise your emotional intelligence, you are more likely to choose a life partner based on similar emotional responses to specific stimuli. Your choice will impact on your overall well-being, which can be measured according to three important gauges, namely health, knowledge, and wealth.

Each of these gauges plays a vital role in the success of any relationship and indeed in your life as a whole.

❖ Health

If your relationship brings you happiness, gives you a sense of direction, has meaning and empowers you with love and a sense of well-being, it is well worth fostering. Good, healthy relationships may foster longevity. If you stay true to yourself, you will remain true to your lover, and your relationship will flourish.

❖ Knowledge

Employ empathy and your emotional intelligence to listen to your partner, interpret their verbal as well as their non-verbal clues about how they feel, and then react in a positive, constructive manner. Let your partner know how you feel through your words, facial expressions and actions. In this way, the relationship is cemented and has a good chance of surviving the unexpected challenges life throws at it.

Let your knowledge about your partner be your guide to handling them with courtesy, care, and empathy. Not everyone responds in the same way, to outward displays of affection or being touched in specific ways. Be sensitive to your partner's needs and expectations without losing your own identity in the process. When you are unsure, don't be afraid or embarrassed to ask before your act.

❖ Wealth

All relationships are like your bank account. Invest in them, and they will grow, flourish, and earn you great rewards. Alternatively, neglect them, and they will wither and eventually die. Being attracted to someone and falling in love is only the beginning of the relationship. The success of the relationship lasting depends on the amount of work you are willing to invest in it. This is a two-way effort by the way. Both parties should invest in their mutual interests in order to ensure the growth and survival of their love.

Let go of past hurts and negative emotions. These are like thieves that come under cover of darkness to steal your treasured love. When partners acknowledge and accept each other's short-comings, they can begin to build positive bridges for a lasting relationship. Remember, the only challenge with making mistakes is in not being able to admit to them. No one is perfect. Mistakes are a way of learning so use these to your advantage rather than hiding from them.

View change as an opportunity to develop your relationship in another direction rather than see it as a negative force. Change presupposes development and growth. Embrace it and use it to your full advantage to grow a healthy, happy relationship.

How Healthy Relationships Affect the Balance in Your Home

In any home, good, healthy, balanced relationships create the fabric for success. When family members work together for the good of the entire unit by providing emotional support and financial well-being, the overall health and potential success of the family improves exponentially. It is good to part of a loving family because there is a strong sense of belonging and a clear understanding of being loved, wanted, and respected.

When conflict and discord are the normal order of the day in a family situation, the health and well-being of the family under these circumstances rapidly disintegrate to leave chaos and destruction in its wake.

Marriage

Marriage is not only a union between two people but between two families. It protects not only the well-being of family members but offers security, companionship, economic security, and emotional support to all its members. A good marriage can be positively linked to promoting health, wealth, and low mortality. Happily married people are generally presumed to take an active, positive interest in each other as well as in each member of their family. They also share the responsibility of raising their family

Positive family dynamics offer social support and the development of deep social and family bonds that have the ability to weather all kinds of unexpected disasters and still hold strong. Children growing up in families of this nature have a better chance of success in their own marriages than those from dysfunctional families because they learn from the good examples of their elders.

Social ties

Married couples and their families very often develop strong social bonds within their families that will last the course of their lifetime. Each family member learns from an early age that they are an essential part of the family unit and, as such, can always depend on their family no matter the circumstances.

The success of a family unit is not necessarily dependent on its financial status, although in many instances, financially independence is a positive factor. Simple, families in which income may be limited, still have strong familial bonds. The members of these families often work twice as hard as their counterparts to ensure each member has security and protection.

Educating children

Family members often stand together for the good of their children. In some instances where a family suffers the death of a parent, extended family members will step in to take on this responsibility. It is through these strong familial bonds that children learn the value of being part of the family unit. Understandably, not all families operate in quite the same positive way. Those that do, develop healthy, lasting relationships with each other while those that don't, seldom survive intact for long.

Increasing security

Healthy family relationships dynamically increase the physical, emotional, as well as the social security for each member. Loving families generally rely on each member for support and advice. There is an underlying trust and acceptance that is hard to destroy. If you think of the Mafia families, for example, although they may not be known for many good deeds, their members certainly stick together in all sorts of circumstances.

Developing Quality Relationships

Although family relationships are of undeniable importance to each member, some families don't foster these relationships to the detriment of the entire family. Healthy relationships that are grown from shared quality time, good communication, and teamwork encourage the development of strong bonds of love and respect. This ensures a sense of security and acceptance between all family members.

Problem-solving and conflict resolution

Family life is not all rainbows and roses, and to believe it is, is to live under a serious misapprehension. However, despite every family's ups and downs, there is often inter-family support and assistance when challenges arise. Joint efforts at problem-solving strengthen familial ties. In many cases, members of the family will stand together in support of one member to assist with conflict resolution. Such families have developed strong, unbreakable bonds that defy the enemy's best efforts.

Unfortunately, when conflict becomes a consistent internal family problem, the chances of the family surviving diminishes rapidly.

Rules and routines

Every successful family has, at its roots, simple rules and routines that ensure the smooth running of the family dynamic. Rules usually provide the outline or boundary within which the family member co-operates in a positive manner with each other. Families without rules and boundaries often end up with family members living in a chaotic mess of unruly behavior without showing respect or empathy for each other.

Quality time together

Modern families are sometimes hard-pressed to share good quality time together because of work, traveling, or other constraints. However difficult this may prove to be, it is essential for family members to enjoy some quality time together on a daily basis. Often the best way to create time together is to share the evening meal at the family table. This bonding time can have a very positive knock-on effect for each member as they get the opportunity to communicate, share ideas and concerns, talk through problems, and discuss future plans. It's also a valuable opportunity to really listen to each other and offer empathy and support. Quality time together forms the foundation for the development of strong familial bonds and a sense of belonging.

Having fun together

As the saying goes: "All work and no play makes Jack a dull boy." Fun, laughter, and relaxation play a vital role in the health of a family. Relaxation is important for recharging your life-battery, and when downtime can be shared with your loved ones, the charge is all the better and lasts longer. Laughter can often be the best medicine for most ailments. A family that laughs and cries together is one that is likely to stay intact. Sharing your intimate emotions with your family members should strengthen rather than perturb you.

Chapter 9: Family Counseling Strategies

Our family, into which we are born or adopted, forms the foundation for our future growth, development, and success in life. From our family, we learn our language, customs, habits, how to behave, which behaviors are unacceptable, respect for our elders, routines, rules, and how to interact with those around us.

If our family is well-balanced with sound, healthy values, and relationships, our future is likely to be built on a similar foundation, and our relationships have a good chance of lasting. The opposite holds true for the dysfunctional family in which there is little or no direction and guidance given to children. Their future is likely to be pretty bleak.

All families experience good and bad times, but it's the way in which the family handles these issues that set them on the road to success or ruin. When family counseling becomes necessary, we look to a family counseling therapist whose work forms a branch of psychotherapy.

The family counseling therapist assists in supporting families in crisis by introducing strategies for change to strengthen and improve existing intimate familial bonds.

A family therapist, the go-to person in this instance, will recommend the most suitable type of support. A wide range of counseling therapies are available. Together we will explore a sampling of them.

Types of Therapies

Structural therapy

Developed by Salvador Minuchin, structural therapy was founded on five important principles:

- ❖ The interpersonal interactions between members of the family take precedence over any individual psyche.
- ❖ An 'identity matrix' is formulated from the observations of the interpersonal relations between family members.
- ❖ The family structure is viewed in terms of its social structure.
- ❖ The success of the interactions within the family and their response to individual needs is indicative of whether it is a well-functioning family or a dysfunctional one.
- ❖ The therapist acts as a catalyst for positive growth and development in the family with the end result being a more unified, well-adjusted family.

This type of therapy relies heavily on the personal interactions of family members because collectively, they form the basic matrix for the family. Salvador Minuchin believes the family is only as strong as its collective whole and that the relationships within the family are what bind the individuals together to create a unit. If these bonds are well developed, the family can be said to be well-functioning. The reverse is obviously true, and in this case, the therapist will assist family members in acknowledging their individual roles within the collective. The therapist will also help them to reinforce the family bonds so they can restructure and strengthen the unit.

Strategic therapy

Strategic therapy consists of a combination of a number of therapies and has five basic tenets:

The brief social stage during which the therapist meets with the parties to assess the situation.

This is followed by the problem stage during which the problem is revealed, and the therapist is given the opportunity to suggest possible solutions.

Thereafter the interactional stage allows for the parties concerned to work together with the therapist in a positive and productive manner, thrashing out the details of the problem and expressing their ideas.

The goal-setting stage is then reached during which the therapist assists the parties in setting realistic goals for the solution to their problem.

This is followed by the task setting stage where specific tasks are set, and the parties are expected to acknowledge their role and take ownership of their joint responsibilities in working towards a mutual resolution.

Systemic therapy

Systemic therapy is an offshoot of family therapy and focuses on the value of language and social influences, which are two basic areas affecting developing relationships. Systemic therapy emphasizes the importance of the inter-effect these relationships have on each other within the framework of the family, the workplace, the sports arena, or the education environment. It believes that individuals cannot be studied or understood in isolation but rather only through their interaction with others within a specific social system. Systemic therapy studies the patterns that develop in these social systems in order to address maladaptive behaviors.

Narrative therapy

Narrative therapy separates the individuals from their problems and encourages them to take responsibility for themselves by making use of their own set of skills to solve their problems. The therapist will guide the patient to develop a new 'story' or narrative about their life that will afford them more of an opportunity for the successful resolution of their challenges.

Transgenerational therapy

This type of therapy involves interviewing the extended family members across generations in order to examine both past and present issues. These issues are then considered in light of the entire family to recognize and acknowledge any problems as well as identify suggestions for possible solutions. Based on the family's history, present challenges are examined through this lens to prevent future repeats of these challenges.

Communication therapy

Communication forms part of the foundation for any healthy relationship, whether that be a relationship between the adults or the parents and their children. Communication is a vital component for the well-being of all families and everyone in the family.

Unfortunately, our modern lifestyle and the advent of electronic devices have degraded communication skills to a large degree. Without healthy, open, and honest communication, family bonds begin to disintegrate, leaving a vacuum in which members exist in isolation.

Communication therapy is valuable in these instances where there is a breakdown in the communication bond between partners, especially in a marriage. Communication can disintegrate due to secrecy issues, unresolved trauma, brutality between partners, and mental health issues, to name but a few. The therapist may address the root causes as well as offer suggestions for the use of different forms of communication channels.

Psychoeducation

This is a useful tool for transferring information and skills to individuals suffering from mental health issues. It aids self-support through knowledge and practice.

Relationship counseling

Modern families are under increased stress now more than ever before. The increasing challenges parents must face with the spiraling cost of living, on-going issues at work, breakdowns in social service, as well as being constantly bombarded by the media cause a great deal of stress in many families. The knock-on effect can result in a breakdown in communication between partners because of financial difficulties, sexual intimacy issues, disobedient children, and a lack of trust and faith.

Relationship counseling is possibly one of the most valuable tools for modern families struggling to reinforce good communication skills in their family in light of the advent of electronic devices that have skewed communication skills drastically.

Chapter 10: Maintaining the Dynamic Balance in the Family

The importance of a well-balanced family that provides parents and children the opportunity to grow and develop within a safe, caring, supportive environment wherein trust, respect, honesty, generosity, and empathy are important values is not something that magically happens in some lucky families.

A lot of information has been written on the value and important role that a healthy, well-balanced family plays in the future successes of the children and the relationship between the parents.

Maintaining a well-balanced family takes hard work, commitment, and a sense of responsibility, and it is the parents' duty to set the foundation for the type of family they would like to raise. So where should parents begin in their quest to create a well-balanced family? Here are a few ideas, in no particular order, to help parents in their quest to develop and grow a happy, healthy, well-balanced family.

Create Structure and Schedules

Some modern parents appear to be afraid of taking control of their families by setting up routines and boundaries for their children. Children generally thrive when they feel secure, and routines can support their sense of security. Trying to keep mealtimes as routine as possible can be a challenge due to parents' work commitments, but every effort should be made to ensure a good sleep routine for the children is established as early as possible.

Planning schedules for the children helps to keep them organized and makes them feel secure. Schedules also assist parents in keeping up with all the sports, extracurricular activities, academic and social events their children are required to attend.

A structured home may sound like a military prison, but it need not be that rigid. The bottom line is that structure keeps the family wheels well oiled and running smoothly. In turn, there is less chance of chaos and more opportunities for good quality family time.

A structured, well-organized home environment with good routines will also foster a good work ethic and assist children in completing their homework in an orderly manner.

Communication Is Key

Communication is a key element to successful family dynamics. When parents set a good example by communicating with their children and then listening attentively to their responses, children learn the importance of this valuable skill. When parents talk to their children rather than at them, they open the channel for the development of good communication skills.

There are, however, considerable challenges to developing good communication skills in the modern family. One of these challenges comes with the advent of exciting, electronic devices that absorb our children's attention. In order to reset the communication clock in the home, there needs to be a firm decision taken by the parents to give devices a 'curfew time.'

There should also be a specific time set aside for quality, family-time when parents and children can sit together to chat about their day and share ideas and concerns, ask questions and garner the support and advice of the family member. Competing with modern electronic devices is a losing battle, so parents should draw the line at some point and take responsibility for making the decision to talk face-to-face. Spending time in each other's company, communicating with each other builds strong familial ties.

Without being pedantic or forceful, parents should think of creative ways to achieve this device downtime with the minimum of fuss. Once children accept the routine of spending 'real-time' together and witness the benefits, they usually are happy to buy into the new plan and spend time together with the family. The secret is to begin this routine as early as possible to that is becomes fully entrenched by the time electronic make their debut.

Family Responsibility

Each member of the family should be given chores for which they are solely responsible. This teaches the children that they are members of the family and that they all need to work together for the good of the family unit. This can sometimes be a challenging task for parents to allocate suitable tasks to the different age groups in the family. However, when managed well, joint responsibility pays dividends in the long run. Children who learn to take responsibility for themselves in their home environment are not afraid to do the same in their school or community.

Remember to not fall into the 'pay-as-you-do' trap where children expect a financial reward for chores they have completed. They need to learn that by being part of the family team, they are required to bring their efforts to the table for the good of the team and not merely for individual gain.

Teach empathy and respect

One of the most important skills parents can impart to their children is that of teaching their empathy. Being able to listen attentively and respectfully to their parents and siblings will enable them to develop a good understanding of each family member. In turn, they will realize they are being accorded the same attention and respect.

Respect for self as well as for others is learned early in life and is a valuable life skill that is unfortunately not given sufficient attention either at home or in the classroom.

Give praise where it is due

Show your children you are proud of their efforts. Starting early in your children's lives, make sure to thank them when they have done good deeds or completed chores well. Tell them how proud you are and how glad you are to have them as members of your family. Praise supports the growth of positive self-esteem and grows the children's sense of worth. It fosters a desire in your children to always give their best efforts.

Acceptance for all

A well-balanced family ensures every member is accepted for they are. Their individual idiosyncrasies are praised and indeed supported. Each family has value, and collectively, they make the family, the happy, successful, and dynamic unit it is.

Parents who are emotionally intelligent and have empathy are good at sizing up each child's strengths and weaknesses. They are able to encourage each child to develop their strengths while offering support for their areas of need.

At no point will any member of the family belittle or make fun of another. The strong familial bond that keeps the members grounded and together.

Developing humor and a positive outlook

Families who can laugh together and share silly moments are usually happy and content in their own skin. When humor is encouraged, it lightens somber moments and brings respite. The news of the world is often so full of doom and gloom. People become depressed hearing about the wars, needless deaths, rises in prices, and everything else. It is wonderful to come home to smiles and cheerful faces.

Setting a good example

Because children learn by example, it behooves parents to take responsibility to live and cooperate within the family structure in such a way that they will be proud to see their children following in their footsteps.

So mom and dad, be the success you want your children to be. This is a tall order for sure, but a very rewarding one. Parenting is a full-time job, and one that has many unforeseen challenges. When parents bond and work together for the good of their family, the outcome can only be successful.

Paying it forward

The family unit

The term 'paying it forward' refers to a beneficiary of a good deed or unexpected windfall, repaying this kindness to others instead of the initial sponsor.

Good family values are taught by responsible parents who acknowledge their obligations to their children. In turn, children who enjoy the privilege of growing up in a well-balanced, caring, supportive, and loving family are able to one day raise children of their own with the same values. Well-functioning families produce well-behaved off-spring that usually show an avid interest in becoming successful adults. In this way, good family values are passed on through the generations.

Personal relationships

The family is the primary unit in which children learn the value of communication, sharing, positive interaction, respect, mutual support, and co-operation.

The members of well-balanced families who have learned empathy and have well-developed emotional intelligence are perhaps capable of forming lasting relationships, identifying potential challenges to these relationships, and addressing these concerns as early as possible. They are in a better position to ensure successful relationships than those people raised in a dysfunctional family unit.

Well-balanced, emotionally intelligent people are more likely to interact positively and to show empathy where it is needed. They pass their knowledge, care, and values on to those with whom they come in contact. In this way, they touch the lives of everyone around them in a positive and constructive way.

The community

Passing on ethical values to the community occurs in schools, churches, at sports venues, and in public places like stores, hospitals, and restaurants.

Well-raised children and adults interact in a positive manner wherever they go. These are often the popular people who others want to be around because it is often a pleasure to be in their company. Their good manners and positive attitudes brush off on those around them.

Paying it forward is a valuable way of passing on good values and teaching others about empathy and the importance of developing healthy emotional intelligence. Not only can these values have a positive knock-on effect for those suffering from anxiety and depression, but people possessing these values are less likely to become victims of a wide array of mental health disturbances.

Chapter 11: How to Use Therapy to Become Your Best Self

Self-help

The best solution is to use the professional services of a CBT therapist. However, therapy may not always be available to everyone. Perhaps you do not have sufficient medical insurance and the cost is excessive, or you may not be able to take time off of work, find transportation to the clinic, or have a CBT therapist in your area.

Do not despair. There are other options available to you. Self-directed therapy can be a moderately effective tool for dealing with anxiety and depression. There are numerous self-help books and dozens of reliable internet sites you can access to obtain valuable information and hints to assist yourself.

The value of self-help therapy is that you can not only measure your progress daily but learn valuable tools and skills that will stand you in good stead for the long-term management of your condition.

Perhaps the most important aspects of self-help therapy are diligence and commitment. Whether you are fortunate enough to be able to enjoy the services of a professional therapist or have to rely on your resources, you will have to show allegiance to your therapy program.

Another valuable aspect to consider is the support of someone such as a loving partner, a trusted family member, or a reliable friend who is willing to act as your confidante and who will encourage you in your quest.

Self-help CBT is becoming more prevalent and has been classed as an important part of 'stepped care.'

Obviously, self-help cognitive-behavioral therapy is not for everyone. The severity of your anxiety and depression disorder will need to be taken into careful consideration before embarking on a self-help regime.

If you are interested in self-administered CBT, the Association for Behavioral and Cognitive Therapists keeps a list of well-researched books and study material that you may find of interest.

Action for Change

We know that suffering from anxiety disorder runs hand-in-hand with depression, and the two conditions in tandem create a great deal of stress. So, how are you going to set about the interesting task of self-help?

Here are some useful guidelines that you can consider.

❖ Learn to identify your thought patterns

Our thoughts govern our actions. Thoughts develop in our conscious mind, which is where we store meaning gathered through our senses as well as thorough knowledge from learning and experiencing. Our rational, reasoning conscious mind forms conclusions and makes decisions. Our thoughts are sorted and processed here before being stored in our subconscious mind, which is known as the seat of memory, instinct, and action.

The subconscious mind is a powerful, complicated repository for all information. It is the seat of our intelligence and the driver of our personal 'vehicle', called self. Our subconscious mind is the source of our emotions and responses to every event we experience. If we can learn to control our subconscious mind, we will, in turn, be successful in controlling our actions, which in turn will have a positive effect on how we live our lives.

❖ Our thoughts affect our behavior

In order to discover how these thoughts affect your feelings and subsequently, your behavior, you need to take stock of which incidents or occurrences in your life drive you to a specific set of behavioral patterns. Because we are emotional beings, it is not easy to separate how we feel from how we act. If, however, we are successful at identifying the triggers for specific emotional responses, we are in a better position to control our emotions.

❖ Our thoughts reflect our behavior

Decide if your thoughts are an accurate reflection of how you really feel. We cannot, unfortunately, divorce our thoughts from our behavior. Our thoughts are sent from our conscious mind to our subconscious mind, where they are interpreted through our actions. When we are in control of what we think, we are able to control our responses and act rationally. The opposite is also true.

When we are angry or sad, we are not always able to control our physical responses to our emotions. This incapacity might lead us to lash out or to cry. Negative and positive thoughts are relayed to the subconscious and replayed through our actions.

❖ Replace biased, negative thoughts with those that are more realistic

The link between our thoughts and our actions is instantaneous and can have far-reaching implications. It is, therefore, vitally important for each of us to seriously consider releasing negative thoughts and prejudices, and replacing these with positive energy.

Negative Energy Versus Positive Energy

Our personal energy is a powerful resource that can be put to good use or bad. Negative thoughts such as anger, jealousy, prejudice, and hatred break us down and create an imbalance in our lives that robs us of fulfilling our potential. Positive thoughts like happiness, acceptance of others, empathy, and love enables us to find 'pockets of peace' in our lives where we can re-energize our souls and minds.

We need to acknowledge our evil thoughts and eradicate them as quickly as possible, for they are breeding grounds for future evil deeds. In instances where evil deeds are not actually committed, negative thoughts have a detrimental effect on our health and well-being. They may materialize in the form of stress, anxiety disorders, or depression.

The answer, which is, of course, easier said than done, is to nullify the negative and build and nurture the positive.

Powerful Tools for building Well-Being and Inner Peace

Inner peace is believed by some people to be an elusive, pie-in-the-sky type of fairy-tale. It is, however, quite attainable, and for those who know its true value and are willing to make some sacrifices in order to attain inner peace, it is worth the effort.

The added bonus of finding inner peace is that it has a knock-on effect for all those who come into contact with the individual who possesses it. Inner peace is the key to flourishing, loving relationships, the development of personal creativity, the formation of strong, lasting, loving family bonds, job satisfaction, and co-operative interaction between colleagues, better, respectful behavior in children, and a generally positive outlook on life.

Two valuable options to building and growing personal well-being and inner peace include:

- ❖ Meditation

Meditation has its roots in Eastern cultures and presupposes the value of self-help through deep, introspective thought that allows the mind to recapture its power and energy when the body is in a state of conscious relaxation.

It is a process that requires consistent repetition and concentration on a specific idea to be of value, and although there are a number of different types of meditation, it is important that you find the best version that works for you.

- ❖ Mindfulness training

Mindfulness training is a fairly recent, more upbeat approach to meditation in which the individual participant remains fully aware of their environment, although they are not perturbed in any way by it. In order words, they are present in body and mind but allow their mind to wander and as it does, they take notice of the thoughts that migrate in and out of their minds.

Mindfulness alludes to the power that one develops when one lives resolutely and utterly in the now. Being mindful means you are alert and aware of your complete environment and all that is in it. When you reach this state of mindfulness, you are capable of responding to all the different nuances in the environment in a more positive and fruitful manner. Your stress and anxiety levels decline accordingly, and this places you in a more receptive position for achieving inner peace of mind.

In order to fully benefit from mindfulness training, you should be prepared to practice focusing on the positives in your world, which will, in turn, assist you in reaching your full potential and living a happier, more abundant life.

The Mindfulness App could be of benefit to parents and primary caregivers in teaching their children to develop lasting stress releasing skills and meditation techniques that are likely to have enduring positive effects for quality, restful sleep-training.

Helpful Technologies

Whether you are dealing with severe depression, deep sadness, loneliness, or grief, you may benefit from the added support of one or more of the following apps. There is a wide variety of technologies available to support training for mindfulness, well-being, and empathy. A few are mentioned below.

1. Aura

Aura offers mini-meditation sessions of about three minutes in duration. Its main aim is to assist individual users with reducing anxiety and stress.

The Aura program app, through the use of a beautiful selection of sounds from nature, offers users the opportunity to keep a gratitude journal and make an attempt to track their moods and take note of what triggers specific reactions.

2. Breethe

Breethe is a simple app used to track users throughout the day, providing support to help stay on track with their specific meditation schedule. It offers tips on how to overcome stressful situations through breathing deeply and focusing on inner peace and letting go of the pressure and negative thoughts.

3. Buddhify

Buddhify is a mindfulness meditation app organized by themes that suit specific times in your daily schedule. It is a popular app for assisting those who have difficulty falling asleep.

4. TalkLife

TalkLife is a valuable app offering sufferers of depression the opportunity to talk freely to others with the same affliction, in a safe and tolerant space. TalkLife supports its users in a similar way to group therapy. Anonymous sharing is encouraged if you are not yet sufficiently confident to disclose your personal details. This app is suitable for use with both iPhone and Android.

5. Daylio Mood-Tracker

The Daylio Mood-Tracker app gives the user an early warning about situations that promote mood swings. The user is encouraged to journal their moods in order to predict potentially harmful situations and to avoid these at all costs. This app is suitable for use with both iPhone and Android.

6. Depression CBT

This is a self-help app based on cognitive-behavioral therapy, uses mood-tracking and motivational aspects to aid the listener in developing more positive thought patterns. This app is ideal for use in the vehicle during the morning and evening commutes. This app is for specific Android use.

7. What's up?

What's up? Is a useful app with its foundation in cognitive-behavioral therapy and acceptance therapy? It offers a variety of breathing exercises as well as grounding techniques and ways to identify skewed thought patterns. There is also a facility to connect to the app's forum.

8. Pacifica

This is an interesting mindfulness app, designed by a psychologist that aims specifically at helping you identify your troubles and feelings. It makes use of the visualization technique as well as mindfulness meditation and systematic relaxation of all your muscles. This app is suitable for use with both iPhone and Android.

9. Calm: Meditation & Sleep

Sleep is a valuable tool to conquer stress and anxiety. The lack of sleep generates increased stress. The more stressed you become, the less likely you are to enjoy a restful snooze. This merry-go-round phenomenon is directly related to depression.

'Calm' is a useful phone app that has been designed to support guided personal meditation. It caters to those individuals who struggle to fall into a deep and restful sleep. Calm also offers the user the opportunity to destress, unwind, and release all the tension that has built up during the day.

Calm has a soporific effect that induces inner peace and a sense of well-being. Calm is used in a number of schools and offers children the opportunity to learn valuable skills in dealing with stress relief. Many children are faced with increasing stress due to the impact of the rush and bustle of modern life. These children require added support in order to help them overcome the challenges of increased stress. Failure to learn useful stress-releasing techniques puts these children at greater risk of early burn-out.

Calm trains the listener to pay attention to and be mindful of their present status. It also helps to develop an awareness of one's inner feelings in order to purposefully consider each feeling's value and the appropriate response.

Calm encourages the listener to actively participate in their search for spaces and places in their lives where they can find a peaceful retreat to meditate. Meditation is an excellent practice to recommend to anyone who needs to find solace and peace.

Conclusion

Therapy can play an important role in assisting you in reaching your full potential. By working to improve yourself, you inadvertently touch the lives, in a very positive way, of everyone with whom you come in contact. Because we are social beings, interactions with other people are part of our daily lives, so if we can make subtle changes for the better in our own lives, these are likely to affect all who know us. Family life will improve as our attitude develops a more positive and empathetic approach to raising our children and interacting with our partner. The quality of our working life will also show an upswing as we practice more empathy and patience toward our colleagues. Life, in general, will be enhanced as we show fewer prejudices and greater acceptance for all whom we meet.

So, where do you begin?

Schedule personal activities that bring you pleasure and a sense of peace: Walk your dogs, run in the park, listen to relaxing music, lie on your back and watch the stars on a clear night. Whatever 'floats your boat' is good! These activities do not have to be time-consuming but should be regular and consistent to ensure your successful progress toward inner peace and harmony.

Take note of how your thoughts affect your emotions and, ultimately, your actions, and make every effort to discard negative thoughts. It is the negative thoughts that drive us to do hasty things for which we are inadvertently sorry afterward. We live in a crazy, violent world where empathy and care for other people hardly exist. For example, if a driver cuts across your lane of traffic, almost hitting your vehicle, instead of yelling and losing your cool, try to breathe deeply and find something positive to focus on, such as rejoicing that he did not hit your car. For the most part, we view strangers with suspicion rather than with interest. Humanity has become so focused on our own individual needs, wants, and pleasures that we have lost sight of the bigger picture and become entrenched in a negative spiral-type existence. Plan events, minor in nature, to begin with, that you can do in your spare time. What spare time you may ask? Well, remember those 'pockets of peace' mentioned earlier? It is important to create a few peaceful gaps in your crazy, chaotic day to 'chill out' and take a break.

Take a good look at what really bothers you in life. Examine the problem as honestly as you can. Sometimes problems are perceived to be bigger and more complicated than they really are. Break the enigma down into more manageable components and then tackle each of these, one-at-a-time. You will soon have the matter under control and be able to move forward with a clear mind and a peaceful heart. So, for example, your mother-law snores loudly and disturbs the entire household every night! If this issue has reached a point where you feel you could do the poor old woman physical harm, stop! Breathe! And consider your more positive options. Perhaps a new cushion that will prop her head up better, or a visit to the clinic for some recommended medication, or purchase ear-plugs for the family, or perhaps a combination of these will be best.

Face your fears and be as honest as you can about these. Then, with professional help or the support of a loving partner or trusted friend, begin to gradually and systematically work at improving yourself and overcoming the fear that haunts you. Fear, as we all know, is a debilitating emotion that slowly whittles away at our confidence until we are nothing more than a shell of our former selves.

Follow the self-help program you have chosen or adhere to the parameters of the professional therapy sessions you attend, as closely as you can. Don't be fooled into deviating from the plan. It is easy to skip out on a few parts of any program when we mistakenly believe we do not require that particular section, or it does not resonate with us.

If we practice this sort of action, we will find the program less beneficial than we had expected.

Complete the program. See it through to its final stage before you decide on its benefits. A good program, whether self-directed or professional, will have a beneficial outcome by lowering your stress levels, providing you with priceless skills, lift your mood, and improve your overall well-being.

References

Anxiety and Depression Association of America, ADAA. Generalized Anxiety Disorder (GAD). (2019). Retrieved from: https://adaa.org/understanding-anxiety/generalized-anxiety-disorder-gad

Cherry, K. (2019, Nov 27). Importance and Benefits of Empathy. Retrieved from https://www.verywellmind.com/what-is-empathy-2795562

Gillian, S.J. (2016, Sep 13). Therapy Without a Therapist. Retrieved from https://www.psychologytoday.com/za/blog/think-act-be/201609/therapy-without-therapist

Goldsmith, B. (2012, Apr 27). 10 Simple ways to find happiness. Retrieved from https://www.psychologytoday.com/us/blog/emotional-fitness/201204/10-simple-ways-find-happiness

Gorrindo, T., & Parekh, R. (2017, July). Retrieved from https://www.psychiatry.org/patients-families/ocd/what-is-obsessive-compulsive

Manson, M. (2019, April 11). 5 Skills to Help You Develop Emotional Intelligence. Retrieved from https://markmanson.net/emotional-intelligence

NIH. Social Anxiety Disorder: More than just shyness. Retrieved from https://www.nimh.nih.gov/health/publications/social-anxiety-disorder-more-than-just-shyness/index.shtml

Selig, M. (2019, Mar 9). Know Yourself? 6 Specific ways to know who you are. Retrieved from https://www.psychologytoday.com/za/blog/changepower/201603/know-yourself-6-specific-ways-know-who-you-are

Shatto, R. (2018, Nov 8). Retrieved from https://www.elitedaily.com/p/does-emotional-intelligence-matter-in-a-relationship-couples-therapists-weigh-in-13113609

Wodele, A., & Solan, M. (2017, July 19). Phobias: Causes, Types, Treatment, Symptoms and More. Retrieved from https://www.healthline.com/health/phobia-simple-specific